3 1336 00248 6703

S0-DTE-424

791.41   Hintz, H
         Horses in the
         movies
                    1500

cop.a

SAN DIEGO PUBLIC LIBRARY

ALWAYS BRING YOUR
CARD WITH YOU.

Horses in the Movies

ALSO BY H. F. HINTZ:

The Horse (with J. W. Evans, A. Borton, L. D. Van Vleck)

Horses in the Movies

H. F. HINTZ

South Brunswick and New York: A. S. Barnes and Company

London: Thomas Yoseloff Ltd

© 1979 by A. S. Barnes and Company, Inc.

A. S. Barnes and Co., Inc.
Cranbury, New Jersey 08512

Thomas Yoseloff Ltd
Magdalen House
136-148 Tooley Street
London SE1 2TT, England

Library of Congress Cataloging in Publication Data

Hintz, Harold Franklin, 1937-
   Horses in the movies.

  Bibliography: pp. 00
  Includes index.
  1. Horses in moving-pictures. I. Title.
PN1995.9.A5H55   791.43′09′0936   77-74115
ISBN 0-498-02119-X

PRINTED IN THE UNITED STATES OF AMERICA

Contents

Acknowledgments

The author wishes to express his thanks to the following individuals and organizations who helped make this book possible: Rex Allen, Appaloosa News, Caroline Bloomquist, Jerry Brown, Cal Poly at Pomona, Cochise Visitor Center and Museum of the Southwest, Collectors Bookstore, Larry Edmunds Bookshop, Dyke Johnson, Sandra Hallet, Sandra Hintz, Madelyn Hintz, Museum of Modern Art of New York City, Old Tucson, Rothschilds of Ithaca, Philip Rutherford, Roy Rogers Museum, Walt Disney Studios, John Wayne, Warner Brothers Studios, and Zane Grey Museum.

Introduction

Horses have long played a very important part in the movie industry and, in fact, were the first motion-picture stars. Leland Standford, a former governor of California, president of Central Pacific Railroad, and a prominent breeder of trotting horses, wanted to prove that a trotter in action had all four feet off the ground simultaneously. He employed Eadweard J. Muybridge to develop a method to show horses in motion. Muybridge worked on Standford's Palo Alto Stock Farm (now the site of Stanford University) during the 1870s and 1880s. He assembled a large crew of engineers and scientists and, after many attempts, finally succeeded in showing horses in motion using a series of cameras placed at short intervals. He studied trotters, Thoroughbreds, draft horses, and dogs, and proved with his moving pictures that trotting and galloping horses did at times have all four feet off the ground.

Thomas Edison started the movie industry in the United States. In 1894 he made a 643-frame movie called *Bucking Bronco*. It showed Lee Martin of Colorado riding Sunfish. In 1896 Edison produced a forty-three-foot film entitled *The Burning Stable*. Four white horses were seen being led from a stable from which smoke was billowing. The forty-five-foot sequel *Fighting the Fire* showed two horse-drawn fire engines arriving at the scene and the firemen trying to extinguish the fire. Edison produced a short film of Western life entitled *Cripple Creek Bar-Room* in 1898. Another 1898 short film was entitled *Elopement on Horseback*. *The Great Train Robbery* (1903) was the first important American drama ever filmed. It was a Western, although it was filmed in New Jersey.

It is easy to understand why horses have been so important and popular in the movies. Ever since man first domesticated horses, perhaps about 3000 B.C., the bond between horse and man has been very strong. But with the invention of the internal combustion engine, the dependence of man on the horse for transportation, labor, and military power greatly decreased and the number of horses was greatly reduced. But man's love for the horse was not decreased.

In the early 1920s (the peak years for numbers of horses in the United States) it was estimated that there were more than twenty million horses. The numbers gradually decreased until in the early 1950s there were less than four million horses in the United States. In the late 1950s the horse population started to increase dramatically because of the use of horse for recreation. By the 1970s it was estimated that there were eight to ten million pleasure horses in the United States. Many experts predict that the horse population will continue to increase.

The ancient Arab proverb "The outside of a horse is good for the inside of man" is still appropriate today. The pleasure horse has enabled many people to take part in healthy outdoor sports and relieve the pressures of modern civilization. Although America has become more sophisticated, less rural, its love affair with the horse has continued. As Dale Robertson said in the opening of the documentary television series "American Horseman," "I figure there are only two kinds of people in the world—those who own horses and those who wish they did."

The horse has been and will continue to be a very important part of the movie industry and American culture.

Advertisement for *Whirlwind* (1933).

of B movies, he went into television and produced several successful Western series. Champion became a television star of his own series, entitled "The Adventures of Champion the Wonder Horse." Autry did not appear in the series. Jim Bannon, Barry Curtis, and Rebel, a dog, were the supporting players.

The original Champion lived to age seventeen. Several horses, such as Old Baldy, Tennessee, Champ Junior, Little Champ, and Wag, all had their chance to play Champion. The producers of the Gene Autry movies did not make elaborate attempts to disguise the different horses. Differences in face and leg markings were obvious. Champion usually had four white stockings but in *Indian Territory* (1950), the right front leg was not white. In *Loaded Pistols* (1949), Champion sometimes had a solid color right rear leg. Color of tail and mane varied from flaxen to dark. Champion Junior was purchased from Charles Auten in 1946 for $2,500 as a four year old. Auten lived in Ada, Oklahoma, and had exhibited his horse Boots in many area rodeos and fairs. He read in a newspaper that Gene Autry was appearing in a Fort Worth, Texas, rodeo and was looking for another horse. He made the trip to Fort Worth and Boots became Champion Junior.

Champion was a well-traveled horse. He made many personal appearances with Autry and sometimes with only his trainer. Following Tony's lead, he visited the White House.

Fritz

The first really important horse hero of the Western movies was William S. Hart's red and white pinto Fritz. Hart is considered by some authorities to be one of the greatest actors of all the early cowboy heroes. He strived for realism in his movies and wanted them to be more than just entertainment. His movies often depicted the close relationship between a cowboy and his horse and their dependence on each other. Hart's love for Fritz is clearly stated in his autobiography, *My Life East and West*. Apparently his affection for the horse was not just a publicity gimmick. In his book Hart states, "I loved every hair of the little scoundrel's hide." One picture of Hart and Fritz in the book is captioned, "The Greatest All-Round Horse

wide variety of tricks taught him by Johnny Agee, such as the hesitation waltz, hula, jitterbug, and to kneel in prayer. And he rescued Gene in many movies such as *Rim of the Canyon* (1949). He even saved Gene twice in *Loaded Pistols* (1948).

But Autry had an attribute that more than made up for his lack of riding ability. He had real business sense and knew how to promote both himself and Champion. With the decline

Gene Autry rode many different Champions. Apparently, relatively little attempt was made to disguise them. Note the different leg markings, face markings, and even color of mane and tail.

©·D·905_17

that Ever Lived." Hart used several horses in his movies, such as a magnificent black stallion named Midnight and a fine black horse named Jack. But he claimed that Fritz was the only horse that could do and did do anything and everything. Although Hart strived for realism, his movies were often overly sentimental. Hart said that *The Narrow Trail* (1917) was conceived and written in his love for Fritz. The horse made the picture a great success. *Pinto Ben* (1924) was also made as a tribute to Fritz and was based on a poem written by Hart. Further evidence of the strong feelings Hart had for Fritz is in the book *Told Under a White Oak*. The book, published in 1922, has the author listed as William S. Hart's pinto pony, Fritz. Hart attempted to write the book as he thought Fritz might say it. Hart tried to portray a tough cowboy, but he must have been one of the most sentimental.

Just how Fritz got to Hollywood appears to be a mystery. One report suggests that he was brought to California from the plains by an Indian named Lone Bear. However, there is no doubt that Hart acquired Fritz in a rather unusual way. Tom Ince, the producer of most of Hart's early movies, owned Fritz, and although Hart repeatedly tried to buy the pony, Ince would not sell. After Hart had negotiated a large raise, the studio asked that he postpone the raise for just one more picture until they could get the booking price raised. Hart said that he would agree to the postponement provided that they would sell him Fritz. Hart calculated that the postponement of the raise cost him $42,500 salary but he claimed, "the old snoozer is worth it."

Fritz was not a big horse. It has been estimated that he weighed about one thousand pounds. But he was strong and durable and could perform many stunts. One of Hart's favorite tricks was the run and throw. Hart would gallop Fritz and then suddenly stop and throw him to the ground. Although Hart regarded it as one of the most dangerous stunts because of the danger of fracturing a bone, he claimed he threw Fritz in almost every picture that he used him. Fritz did a variety of dangerous stunts such as jumping through windows and over fire. During the filming of *The Toll Gate* (1920) in Tuolumne County, Fritz and

The sentimental William S. Hart.

William S. Hart and Fritz.

30

Grave of Fritz on the William S. Hart Ranch in Newhall, California.

Hart were almost killed doing a stunt. Hart and Fritz were supposed to swim upstream in a swift current but they got into a whirlpool and almost drowned. According to Hart only Fritz's strength and courage and help from the Lord saved them. Hart claimed that he never used a live double for Fritz. This was probably because of his faith in Fritz's ability and because Fritz's distinctive markings and individuality made it difficult to obtain an adequate double. However, in the filming of *Singer Jim McKee* (1924) the horse was to gallop off the edge of a cliff and tumble down to the bottom of the gorge about 150 feet below. Fortunately for Fritz, Hart decided it was too dangerous. Hart rode Fritz to the cliff's edge but he rode an elaborately constructed dummy to the bottom. The dummy was painted to look just like Fritz and was animated by pulling on piano wires. The filming was realistic enough that many people wrote in protesting such treatment of a horse. Hart had to explain that it was a fake horse and even went

to New York City to show a film of how the stunt was conducted to avoid censorship.

Fritz was particularly fond of a mare named Cactus Kate. It was claimed that Fritz worked much better when Kate was around. For example, one day during the shooting of *Travelin' On* (1921) Fritz refused to perform until Kate was brought to the set. The mare was difficult to control and used only in bucking scenes, but nevertheless Hart bought her as a companion for Fritz when he realized Fritz's attraction to her. Fritz also enjoyed the company of Lisbeth, a giant mule. Such attachments between animals are not unusual. Many race horses have ponies, goats, or dogs as mascots or companions. The horses may become highly agitated if the companions are taken away. For example, Seabiscuit was fond of a lead pony named Pumpkin and a dog named Pocatello. Dan Patch liked a small Yorkshire terrier named Little Patch.

Hart started working with Fritz in 1914. Fritz appeared in many of Hart's movies, but because of some disagreements between Hart and Tom Ince, who was reported by Hart to dislike Fritz,

31

Fritz missed fifteen movies but returned in 1919 to appear in *Sand*. Fritz was retired in 1924 after the filming of *Singer Jim McKee* and thus did not appear in *Tumbleweeds* (1925), Hart's last and one of his finest films. Fritz lived the rest of his life on Hart's ranch in Newhall, California. He died at the age of thirty-one. His grave on Hart's ranch* is marked with a large stone and the engraving reads, "Wm. S. Hart's Pinto Pony Fritz—A Loyal Comrade."

KoKo: "The Miracle Horse of the Movies"

Rex Allen, "The Arizona Cowboy," was one of the last successful singing cowboy stars. His striking, well-trained horse contributed greatly to his success. KoKo was a crossbred Quarter Horse and Morgan from Mexico, Missouri. Glenn Randall had originally purchased him for Dale Evans, but it was decided a less spirited horse might better suit her needs. Allen bought him in 1950 for $2500. The horse's cocoa-colored body with light honey-colored mane and tail made him especially effective in technicolor movies. In fact, it was KoKo's different color that first attracted Allen's attention. KoKo appeared in more than two dozen Westerns with Allen, including *Arizona Cowboy* (1950), *Under Mexicali Stars* (1950), *The Overland Trail* (1953), and the *Phantom Stallion* (1953). *Rodeo King and the Senorita* (1951) was a remake of Rogers's *My Pal Trigger* (1946). Most of his movies were filmed during 1950 to 1955. KoKo was retired from public appearances in 1963 after he got into a grain bin and became badly foundered. He spent his retirement at Allen's Diamond X Ranch in southern California, where he died in 1968 at the age of twenty-eight. He was buried in Rex Allen's home town, Willcox, Arizona, at the Cochise Visitor Center and Museum of the Southwest. The grave site has become a popular tourist attraction. The plaque reads:

> "KoKo" Rex Allen's stallion co-star in 30 motion pictures. Traveled over half million miles with Rex in U.S. and Canada. Billed as "The Most Beautiful Horse in the World." At rest here, "Belly High" in the green grass of horse heaven.

*Hart's ranch in Newhall California was willed to the State of California and his home was made into a museum.

Allen continues to raise horses and presently still has two of KoKo's offspring on his ranch.

Allen used a horse named KoKo, Jr. in his post-1963 appearances.

Rex: "King of the Wild Horses"

Rex was the most famous of the horse stars that frequently played wild stallions. Legend says that Rex was found by Chick Morrison, a Hollywood trainer, in a box stall on a ranch near Golden, Colorado. The horse was confined because he had killed a young boy and nobody could handle him. Morrison told Fat Jones that the horse would make a great star. At that time, Jones owned the largest stable in the business of renting horses for the movies. Jones sent Jack Lindell, one of Hollywood's greatest horse trainers, to help Morrison bring Rex back. The purchase price for the black Morgan stallion was reported to be $150. As Morrison prophesized, Rex became a great star and was one of Hollywood's leading money-makers. He starred in a series of silent movies as a wild horse in the twenties and made several talkies in the early thirties. I am not sure that Rex ever actually killed someone, but by all reports, he never

Rex Allen and KoKo.

Rex starred in serials with Rin-Tin-Tin, Jr.

became a gentle horse. Fat Jones was quoted as saying, "He never got to where you could trust him. He was mean to the end." Fred Jackman, a cameraman-director said, "Rex had no particular intelligence, he was mean and undependable, but he responded enthusiastically to certain objectives with definite impulses. For example, if we wanted him to leave the scene quickly, we just showed him another stallion off the set and he would streak to him." Doubles were used for Rex in close-up scenes with actors because any actor with any sense was hesitant to work close to Rex.

He appeared in movies for about fifteen years. His first movies were made by Hal Roach Studios. On January 27, 1927, the *New York Times* reported that Rex was sold to Universal Picture Corp. It was said to be the first transfer of an animal featured in motion pictures. Some of Rex's movies were *Black Cyclone* (1925), *Hoofbeats of Vengeance* (1928), *Harvest of Hate* (1929), *Wild Beauty* (1927), *Plunging Hooves* (1929), *Vanishing Legion* (1931), *Smoky* (1933), and *Wild Blood* (1932). His co-stars included Bob Custer, Guinn (Big Boy) Williams, Hugh Allain, Yakima Canutt, Jack Perrin, Harry Carey, Victor Jory, Frankie Darro, and William Janney.

Rex also co-starred with Rin-Tin-Tin, Jr. in serials such as *The Law of the Wild* (1934) and *Adventures of Rex and Rinty* (1935).

Billboard Magazine had the following comments about Rex's performance in *Smoky*: "This horse is a great deal more intelligent than some human actors we have seen and he is a

credit to the screen. The beautiful animal goes through his paces before the camera and creates a place for himself on the silver screen."

Silver: "That Great White Horse"

Horses ridden by Buck Jones, The Lone Ranger, Sunset Carson, and Hoot Gibson were named Silver.

Many Western film buffs feel that Buck Jones's original Silver was the top action horse of all the B movie stars. They claim he had poise and was perfectly trained. Buck Jones's philosophy of Western movies was more like that of William S. Hart than that of Tom Mix or Ken Maynard. Thus, his horse played a more realistic role than those played by Tony and Tarzan. Silver never got the fattened roles enjoyed by the later horses. Jones wanted action but not a lot of cute stunts.

Jones never cantered over the desert singing to Silver. He didn't like singing cowboys. He said, "They use 'em to save money on horses, riders, and ammunition." He liked to say, "I am an old-time cowboy, the sort the kids used to want to grow up to be like." Jones had several Silvers, and at least four different horses were used as lead horses. They were grays, not white horses, and of course, the gray horse lightens in color as he becomes older. Thus, when looking at pictures of Jones and his horses a wide range of color—dark dapple gray to almost white—can be seen.

The original and the second Silver both lived for over twenty years. The original Silver died in 1940 at the age of twenty-six. The third Silver was retired in the late 1930s and the fourth Silver's last movie was *Dawn on the Great Divide* (1943).

Jones claimed that he bought the original Silver from a rancher for one hundred dollars. It was also claimed that although Silver was a very intelligent horse and easily trained, he wouldn't nicker on cue. Another horse's voice was dubbed in everytime Silver was supposed to nicker.

The titles of the Jones and Silver movies, as was the case of most B westerns, often sounded like they were straight from the pulp magazines. Some examples are *The Boss Rider of Gun Creek* (1936), *The Ivory Handled Gun* (1935),

Buck Jones and Silver.

Ken Maynard and Tarzan.

career. He left the ministry to become an actor in 1921. He died in 1928 after a short illness. He was similar to Tom Mix in that he wanted a lot of action and stunts in his movies. He also gave big parts to his horse, Silver King, a large gray Irish hunter that Thomson bought in New York City. Silver King saved Fred from outlaws and Indians and the schoolmarm. In *Silver King Comes Through* (1927), he won the big race and saved the ranch. In *Thundering Hoofs* (1924), Silver King fought a giant bull. Like many human actors, King was also temperamental. Raymond Lee in *Not So Dumb* claimed that Silver King hated the doubles that Thomson rode and tried to attack them. He also claimed that Silver King suffered from temporary blindness caused by the bright movie lights but recovered when cold cabbage leaves were

applied to the eyes. Silver King ranks with Tony and Fritz as one of the early movie horse greats.

Tarzan: "The Wonder Horse"

Ken Maynard's palomino has not received as much publicity as Fritz and Tony in recent years and many feel that his ability has been underestimated. A major source of information about Tarzan is a series of three articles written by Jon Tuska in *Views and Reviews*. Tuska claimed, "No other horse in the movies, not even Tony, has proven the equal of the original Tarzan, a sensitive nearly human creature that strangely and perfectly complemented Ken's screen personality."

Of course, like any star, Tarzan had his detractors. Frank Manchel in *Cameras West*

"THERE's a product....that LISTERINE TOOTH PASTE...
I have never used a dentifrice that made my teeth feel and look so
clean. And in my business that's important!" Ken Maynard

He could afford $25
for his tooth paste
...he pays 25¢

ONCE again you find a man accustomed to
every luxury using, by choice, that dentifrice which costs him but 25¢.

Once again you find a man whose profession
demands sound and attractive teeth, using Listerine Tooth Paste.

What's the reason? Better results, nothing
more. Millions of people have found that
Listerine Tooth Paste is amazingly superior.
If you haven't tried it, do so now.

See how thoroughly it cleans teeth. See how
it sweeps away ugly discolorations. See the
brilliant lustre and gloss it imparts to the
teeth. Note that wonderful feeling of mouth
freshness and invigoration that follows its use.
Give it a trial now. Your druggist will supply
you. LAMBERT PHARMACAL COMPANY,
St. Louis, Missouri.

REGULAR SIZE - 25¢
DOUBLE SIZE - 40¢

Advertisement with Ken Maynard and Tarzan.

wrote, "Tarzan had poor vision, and Maynard often used doubles for his mount in order to avoid riding straight into a tree."

Tarzan was a half Arabian-half American Saddle Horse that Maynard purchased for fifty dollars at Newhall, California, in 1926 when Tarzan was ten years old. Soon after, Edgar Rice Burroughs visited Maynard's ranch and, according to Maynard, suggested that Ken name it after Burroughs's jungle hero. Later on, the Burroughs's organization objected to Maynard's use of the name, and particularly to a movie, *Come on Tarzan* (1932), but the court allowed Maynard to continue to use the name.

Tarzan was very easy to train and performed a wide variety of tricks. Maynard enjoyed writing in tricks in the scripts and giving Tarzan plenty of opportunity to demonstrate his talents. Tarzan would dance, bow down, roll over and play dead, nod his head in response to questions, and ring fire bells. He saved Maynard from fire, quicksand, outlaws, and Indians and even saved Ken from being dragged to death by a runaway

horse. Tarzan often received acclaim from reviewers. In 1932, *Parents Magazine* wrote, " . . . boys will enjoy the constant action and the hero's remarkably intelligent horse in *Fighting Through*."

Tarzan, according to some reports, was a better performer in the silent than in sound movies. He had been trained to obey verbal commands and never was quite able to adjust to other types of commands. Of course, doubles were used for Tarzan. At one time, Maynard had a stable of eight Palomino horses that he used in the movies. In one movie, *Six Shootin Sheriff* (1930), the original Tarzan was not used at all even though he received billing. He was traveling with Maynard's road show and did not return to Hollywood until the six-day filming was completed. Tarzan's last movie was *Lightning Strikes West,* released in 1940. He apparently died shortly after the movie was completed. Maynard buried him "beneath an elm tree somewhere in the Hollywood hills," but he never revealed the exact location. In fact, he tried to keep Tarzan's death a secret and wouldn't admit that the animal had died until several years after Tarzan's death. By the 1940s Maynard was having a lot of problems, including excess weight and excess alcohol, and it was difficult for him to obtain parts in movies. He toured the country with a white stallion named Tarzan II and tried to make a comeback in the movies but was never really successful. Interestingly, several books state that Tarzan was a white horse. But the black and white photography in the early films was of such quality that light palominos such as Tarzan might appear white.

Tony: "The Wonder Horse"

Tom Mix, often called the most popular Western star who ever appeared on the screen, was one of the first to emphasize the horse and glamorize the relationship between the cowboy and his horse. The Tom Mix approach was much more light-hearted than that of William S. Hart, his chief competition. Mix wanted a lot of action with a plot that did not require the audience to expend a lot of effort thinking. Mix was a real showman and an excellent rider. Hence, Tony was given many opportunities to

Tom Mix and Tony.

demonstrate his ability. For many years, he was without doubt the most well-known of all the B horse heroes. However, few of Mix's movies remain, and they are seldom seen on television. Hence, many of the younger generation are not familiar with Tony, although they are acquainted with several of the other horses such as Trigger, Champion, and Topper that appeared on television. In a recent survey of five hundred college students, not one knew that Tom Mix's horse was named Tony, yet more than half of the students named Roy Rogers's horse and several recalled the name of Gene Autry's horse.

Tom Mix bought Tony from Pat Crisman for six hundred dollars when Tony was two years old. It turned out to be a real bargain for Mix, but Crisman also made a profit. He paid less than twenty dollars* to a street vendor for Tony when he was six months old. Crisman reportedly first observed Tony as a colt, following his mother down the streets of Los Angeles as the mare pulled the vendor's cart. I wonder if the vendor ever realized what became of the colt.

Tony's breeding is not known. It has been suggested that he had Thoroughbred and perhaps Percheron blood but that hardly seems likely. His dam was reported to be a range-bred mare from Arizona.

Tony was a true celebrity and received fan mail all his own. One letter from a fan in

*Various articles reported the price to be $12.50, $15.00, $17.50, and $18.00. John Baxter in *Stunt* suggested that Tony might have come from the Miller's Brothers 101 Ranch.

Advertisement for *My Pal, the King* (1932).

Lansing, Michigan, was addressed, "Just Tony, Somewhere in the U.S.A." It arrived at Tom's ranch without difficulty.

Tony's first movie was *Cupid's Round Up* (1918). Not only was he popular but it did not take very long for his importance to be realized.

Tony learned tricks easily. Mix boasted that he did not train Tony, he just simply showed him what to do.

He was one of the most well-traveled horses the world has ever seen. It was claimed that he visited every state in the Union, Mexico, Canada, and Europe. He even called upon President and Mrs. Warren G. Harding at the White House.

Mix was a showman and enjoyed publicity. The book *The Movies* by R. Griffith and A. Mayer illustrates an excellent example of the type of publicity efforts developed for Tony. Tony is shown getting a manicure and permanent wave in preparation for his appearance at the Paramount Theater in New York City. Tony had his hoofprints imprinted in the

Tom Mix and Tony, Jr. appeared in many commercials.

Tom Mix and photo of Tony taken at the time of Mix's death in 1940. Tony died two years later.

sidewalk in front of Grauman's Chinese Theater.

He was retired from pictures in 1932. During his last picture, the aging Tony stumbled and Mix was slightly injured. It was decided that Tony would have to be replaced. Tony was one of the few horse heroes to outlive his master. Mix was killed in an automobile accident in 1940. Tom's will provided that Ivan D. Parker, a Hollywood attorney and horseman, be given charge of Tony. By the fall of 1942, Tony had failed badly. He was taken from Parker's ranch and returned to the Old Mix Estate, where he could die in the stall he had occupied for so many years. On October 10, 1942, a veterinarian chloroformed him in order that he could die without pain and more suffering. Thus, he died at the age of thirty-two.

Prior to the acquisition of Tony, Tom frequently used a roan named Old Blue in his movies and Wild West shows. Tom was quite fond of Old Blue, and when he died, Mix had him buried in Mixville (Tom's combination California ranch and movie studio). He had a wooden pillar with projecting beam constructed over the grave so that daily he could hang a wreath of flowers.

In many of his later movies Mix used Tony, Jr. He bought Tony, Jr. from a florist in the state of New York in 1930. His sire was reported to be an Arabian stallion. Thus, to destroy another press agent's story, Tony, Jr. was really not the son of Tony.

Tony was a magnificent chestnut horse with a narrow white stripe and snip and white stockings on the hind legs, but Tony, Jr.'s markings

This picture of Tom Mix has appeared in many books. It is usually captioned Tom Mix and Tony, but it is really Tom Mix and Tony, Jr.

were even more striking. He had a wide white stripe on the face and four white stockings. I have seen several books containing pictures captioned "Tom Mix and his famous horse Tony," but usually the horse has four white stockings. Perhaps pictures of Tony, Jr. were more plentiful or, perhaps because of the white markings, the pictures were more pleasing to the editors. Nevertheless, several books contain pictures of Tony Jr., calling him Tony. Both horses were well muscled and had similar conformation, although some more modern horse judges might suggest that Tony was on the small size and a bit straighter in the shoulder and thicker in the neck than might be desired. Tony Jr. was also popular with the critics. The movie critic of the *New York Times* when reviewing *The Terror Trail* in 1933 wrote that "Tony Jr. was as fine a bit of horse flesh as ever breathed."

Mix had many other horses. He usually kept at least 25 horses on his TM Bar Ranch. He also used Comanche, a large palomino, in parades. He had a pinto named Apache, a trick mule

named Jasper, a bay hunter named Ponca, and mares named Nina, Doe, Clara Bow, Banjo, and Betty Lou. Many of the animals were used in Mix movies or rented to other studios. Mix also used a large white horse named Tony II in many parades.

Topper

"I ride my horse Topper, chase rustlers and outlaws, shoot my six shooters and do the things that every kid and man in America would want to do." Topper made his film debut in 1935 when William Boyd started the Hopalong Cassidy series. He appeared in sixty-six "Hoppy" westerns and many television films. In fact, it was the television industry that brought Boyd and Topper their greatest fame. In the early fifties they were among the most popular of all television stars. Their names and pictures appeared on almost everything that a youngster might buy: comic books, bread, ice cream, clothes. In 1950 there were 108 licensed manufactures of products worth seventy million dollars. Boyd and Topper appeared on the cover of *Time* magazine on November 27, 1950 and the cover of *Look* magazine on August 29, 1950.

Boyd took his role as Hopalong very seriously. He tried to project an image that kids could admire and emulate. As he said to his young admirer, Jay, in *Renegade Trail* (1939), "Play fair and help folks when they need you."

When Boyd first played in the Hopalong series, he did not particularly like horses, was, in fact, afraid of them. But Boyd's attitude and ability changed as he became more involved with the Hopalong characterization. Boyd tried to make himself and Topper available to youngsters as much as possible. They made several national tours. They visited orphanages and hospitals. For example, in 1953 Topper celebrated his nineteen birthday complete with carrot-topped cake with seventy-five crippled youngsters in a New York hospital.

Topper was a magnificent white animal, but he was not a trick horse. His biggest scene was usually during the final chase when he and Hoppy would capture the crooks. Topper appeared in all of Boyd's Hopalong films, but in

Hopalong Cassidy and Topper.

the later television films much of the heavy work was performed by one of his six understudies.

For many children growing up in the fifties, Hopalong and Topper were the epitome of all cowboy-horse partnerships.

Trigger: "Smartest Horse in the Movies"

Roy Rogers, "The King of the Cowboys," was listed as the No. 1 Western star in the *Motion Picture Herald* poll from 1942 until 1954, when the poll was discontinued. Rogers gives much credit to his beautiful Palomino, Trigger, for his tremendous success. He was quoted by Anthony Amaral as saying, "I have no illusions about my popularity. Just as many fans are interested in seeing Trigger as they are in seeing me." Trigger, billed as "The Smartest Horse in the Movies," was superbly trained by Glenn Randall. Randall taught Trigger more than thirty tricks that were performed upon

word commands and fifty more on other cues.

Rogers purchased Trigger from the Hudkin Bros. Stable for $2,500 in 1938. It is claimed that Trigger originally came from the Santa Susana ranch of Ray "Crash" Corrigan. His original name was Golden Cloud. His dam was a Quarter Horse, and his sire was a Thoroughbred. Trigger was 15.2 hands tall and weighed about 1,100 pounds.

Trigger and his understudies had vital roles and performed elaborate stunts to save Roy and his comic sidekick, usually portrayed by George "Gabby" Hayes. Of course, his roles were often fattened to please his fans. The reviewer for *Variety*, when reporting on *Far Frontier* (1949), said, " . . . tossed in for added kiddie interest are some smart tricks by Trigger," and when reviewing *Spoilers of the Plains* (1951) said, " . . . good use is made of Trigger." Trigger trapped the outlaws in *Utah* (1945), did a dance in *Don't Fence Me In* (1945), and saved Roy when the cowboy was left for dead by

Roy Rogers and Trigger.

Buttermilk was also the name of a buckskin ridden by William Smith in the "Laredo" television series.

Cactus

This bald-faced chestnut was ridden by Neville Brand in the *Laredo* television series.

Copper

Eddie Dean was another of the singing cow-

Eddie Dean and Copper.

boys of the late forties and early fifties who didn't quite reach big-time stardom. However, he did have a beautiful palomino horse named Copper.

Diablo

This pinto was ridden by Duncan Renaldo in the Cisco Kid movies and television films. Renaldo said that Diablo lived to be more than forty years of age. Diablo was trained by Ralph McCutcheon.

Duke

At least two stars rode horses named Duke. John Wayne appeared in a series of six movies for Warner Brothers starting in 1932 in which Duke, the "Miracle Horse," received almost as much billing as Mr. Wayne. Duke, a large white horse, although not a trick horse in the manner of Tarzan or Tony, was, nevertheless, used to rescue Wayne.

Tim Holt rode a brown American Saddle Horse gelding named Duke prior to World War II. Duke's real name was Strike, and he was the son of Ten Strike. His first movie was *Wagon*

Duncan Renaldo as The Cisco Kid on Diablo and Leo Carrilo as Pancho on Lobo.

49

Train (1940), and it might be said that he was an instant success. Holt bought Duke just nine weeks before the filming was to start. Jack Lindell was given the job of training him. By the time the cameras started to roll, Duke could open doors, roll barrels, and knock the gun out of the bad guy's hand with his front feet. Duke was used in several movies such as the *Fargo Kid* (1940), *Along the Rio Grande* (1941), *Robbers of the Range* (1941), and *Cyclone on Horseback* (1941) and performed admirably for Holt. In several of the movies such as *Bandit Ranger* (1942), Duke did not do any tricks, but he was certainly an active, attractive horse. Duke's one big fault was that he hated dogs. It was claimed that whenever he saw a dog, he became difficult to control and would try to kill the dog. By the time Holt returned from World War II, Duke was past his prime, and Tim started riding a palomino named Lightning.

Dynamite

Another horse that was billed as "The Wonder Horse" was Dynamite. A pinto, he costarred with John Preston in *Timber Terror* (1935). A white horse named Dynamite co-starred with Jack Hoxie in movies such as *Gold* (1932). A reviewer for *Parents Magazine* wrote, "*Gold* is a usual western in which a horse figures. The cowboy and his horse trap a gang of thieves."

Lobby card for Buster Crabbe and Falcon.

Falcon

Buster Crabbe was an Olympic swimming champion in 1932. His most famous movie roles were probably as Tarzan and Flash Gordon. He also made more than fifty Westerns, including a series as Billy the Kid during the late thirties through 1948. He used Falcon in many of these Westerns. In the fifties Crabbe starred in "Captain Gallant of the Foreign Legion" television series.

Flash: "The Marvel Horse"

Leo Maloney appeared with Flash and several horses during the 1920s. Monte Cristo and Senator also had billing in Maloney's movies. Another white horse named Flash, "The Wonder Horse," received billing with Gary Cooper in *Arizona Bound* (1927), *The Last Outlaw* (1927), and with Lane Chandler in *Open Range* (1927), Jack Holt also appeared with a horse named Flash in several movies in the 1930s.

Joker

Andy Devine rode this bay horse in the "Wild Bill Hickok" television series. Andy played Jingles, Wild Bill's sidekick.

Knight

This palomino was ridden by Rod Cameron. Cameron appeared in many Westerns starting in 1939. He also starred in non-Western television series in the 1950s.

Tim Holt and the American Saddlehorse Duke, in 1940.

Lobo

This Palomino was ridden by Leo Carrillo in the Cisco Kid film series

Lightning

Pete Morrison used a brown horse named Lightning in the 1920s. In the thirties Morrison was demoted to playing the heavies. Lightning was the name of a wild stallion in a movie of that name that was a Zane Grey adaptation. The human stars were Jobyna Ralston and Robert Frazer. Lightning was also the name of the race horse in *The Reivers* (1969) and the name of the palominos ridden by Tim Holt in his post-World War II Westerns such as *Saddle Legion* (1951). Prior to the war, Holt rode a horse named Duke.

Meadowlark: "The Wonder Horse"

Yakima Canutt was seldom cast as the hero. He usually played the villain, and doubled doing the stunts for the star. In later years he was a second unit action director. However, in at least one movie (*Ridin' Comet,* 1925) he was the good guy and shared billing with a horse named Meadowlark. Canutt also shared billing with Rex, "The King of the Wild Horses."

Midnight

This was a common name for black horses. William S. Hart rode a Midnight in *On the Night State* (1914) and in *The Bargain* (1914). Tim McCoy also rode a black horse named Midnight. In the serial *Overland with Kit Carson* starring Bill Elliot, the villain Pegleg was killed by a stallion named Midnight. Midnight was played by a horse named Blackie owned and trained by Ralph McCutcheon.

Mike

George O'Brien was another of the stars who entered the movie business as a stunt man. His first starring role was in John Ford's *The Iron Horse* (1924). He rode Mike in many of his B Westerns filmed in the thirties. O'Brien also had parts in later Ford films such as *She Wore a Yellow Ribbon* (1949) and *Cheyenne Autumn* (1964).

Monte Cristo

Monte Cristo was one of the horses that received billing with Leo Maloney (*see* Flash). He was in movies such as *Blind Trail* (1926) and *Without Orders* (1926).

Pal

Several horses were named Pal. A white horse named Pal received billing in a Tim McCoy movie (*Rusty Rides Alone,* 1933). Hoot Gibson was not normally identified with one horse but he co-starred with a horse named Pal in a few movies. Gibson also used horses named Midnight, Mutt, Goldie, Starlight (in *Swifty,* 1936), and Pride of Oregon.

Papoose

This was the name of Little Beaver's horse. Little Beaver was the young Indian side-kick of Red Ryder. Several different horses were used. Actors that played Little Beaver included Tommy Cook, Bobby Blake (later the star of television's "Barretta"), Little Brown Jug, and Don Kay Reynolds.

Pardner

Buddy Roosevelt and Pardner made a series of Western movies for the Pathe Studios in the 1920s. Roosevelt was another of the silent stars who couldn't become a star in talkies. However, he was successful in supporting roles and bit parts. For example, he was a rancher in *Stagecoach* (1939). Pardner was also the name of Monte Hale's horse. Hale was a singing cowboy who started making movies in 1944. He retired from the screen in 1951. The Riders of the Purple Sage often provided the backup music in Hale movies.

Raider

Charles Starrett appeared in many movies but he received his greatest fame as the Durango

Kid, the masked rider. The white Arabian, Raider, was a good match for the Kid, who was dressed all in black. The masked costume also had another benefit for Starrett. In the later movies Jock Mahoney doubled for him and did most of the riding and the mask made such deceptions easy to do.

Rebel

Johnny Mack Brown was one of the most popular Western stars in the thirties and forties. He was one of the few leading men to reach the top ten Western stars who didn't have a highly publicized horse. He rode many horses throughout his career, but his favorite was the palomino named Rebel. Rebel was also the name of a white horse ridden by Reb Russel in the 1930s.

Ring-eyed Nellie

Smiley Burnette was one of the few side-kicks who had a featured horse. Nellie frequently

The Durango Kid (Charles Starret) and Raider.

Johnny Mack Brown in *Bad Man From Red Butte* (1940).

52

Johnny Mack Brown on Rebel. His sidekicks are Max Terhune (left) and Raymond Hatton (right).

Smiley Burnette and Ring-eyed Nellie.

demonstrated more sense than Smiley. Burnette frequently used Nellie in Charles Starrett and Gene Autry movies.

Robin Hood

Jack Holt was a cowboy star of considerable talent. He had a long career and appeared in a wide variety of adventure roles. He often starred in movies adapted from Zane Grey novels. In 1923 he appeared in *The Tiger's Claw* in which the horse Robin Hood also received billing. He also frequently appeared with a horse named Flash.

Rocky

Ken Maynard's younger brother, Kermit, also made many Western movies. He usually did stunt work or played the heavy, but he starred in a series for Ambassador Pictures in the thirties with a palomino, Rocky.

Rush

Lash LaRue used not only guns and horses to

53

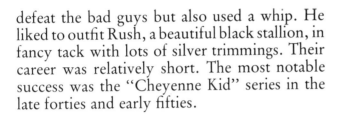

Lash LaRue and Rush.

Whip Wilson and Silver Bullet.

defeat the bad guys but also used a whip. He liked to outfit Rush, a beautiful black stallion, in fancy tack with lots of silver trimmings. Their career was relatively short. The most notable success was the "Cheyenne Kid" series in the late forties and early fifties.

Say Yes

This Thoroughbred was trained by Laurose Tremble and used in the Stronghart (the dog) movies.

Scout

Jack Hoxie, one of top stars from 1922 to 1932, often appeared with a dog named Bunk and horses named White Fury, Dynamite, or Scout. Scout, a white horse, was the one used most frequently by Hoxie. Scout was also the name of Tonto's horse in the "Lone Ranger" series. Actors who played Tonto included Victor Daniels (Chief Tundercloud) and Jay Silverheels.

Senator

Senator was one of the horses teamed with Leo Maloney (*see* Flash).

Silver Bullet

This white horse was ridden by Whip Wilson.

Wilson appeared in forty features during a six-year period starting in 1948. But the movies were quickies and neither Silver Bullet nor Wilson achieved great popularity.

Smoky

Franklyn Farnum used a horse named Smoky in the early 1920s. Three movies have been based on the Will James novel of Smoky the cow horse. Dick Foran had a Smoky in the 1930s. *Parents Magazine,* when reviewing *California Mail* (1937), said, "The singing of Dick Foran and the performance of the horse Smoky are outstanding."

Snowball

This white stallion starred in several silent movies for the Bison Pictures starting in 1910. Many of Snowball's movies were filmed in Griffith Park in Los Angeles. He was purchased by Fred Balshofer for one hundred dollars from a Mexican horse dealer.

Snowflake

This white mare was ridden by Texas Guinan. Texas starred in numerous Westerns before retiring to the nightclub business. Her pictures usually had simple plots and a lot of horse action. Fat Jones said that Texas's favorite horse was Sunny Jim, a horse that was killed performing a movie stunt. The rider was supposed to jump onto a moving train but got Jim too close and the train hit him.

Sonny

Bill Elliot was another one of the top Western stars who did not have a special horse. He bred and raised horses and used one of his own horses, Sonny, in his movies. But he never tried to make Sonny a star à la Champion and Trigger. Elliot rode several movie horses such as Stormy Night, a beautiful gray Quarter Horse (*The Fabulous Texan* 1947).

Star

This horse worked with either Richard Hatton and Marilyn Mills or both in several silent Westerns in the 1920s. Star often saved the hero

Wild Bill Elliot, shown here with Gabby Hayes in *Outlaw Buster* (1943), had several horses but never tried to develop one into a star.

and heroine in movies such as *My Pal* (1924), *The Rip Snorter* (1925), *Range Justice* (1925), *Tricks* (1925), and *Horse Sense* (1924).

Starlight

Starlight and Jack Perrin were one of the most prolific teams in the early cinema. They made at least thirty films during the twenties and several in the thirties. One of their movies was *Starlight, The Untamed* (1926). An interesting review of Starlight's work appeared in *Billboard*. The critic reviewed *Hair Trigger Casey* (1936) and wrote, "Starlight, the Wonder Horse, deserves better support than this." Starlight was also the name of a white stallion ridden by Bob Livingston, and a palomino ridden by Hoot Gibson.

Sunset

Jimmy Wakely rode Sunset in the forties and fifties. Wakely could probably sing as well or better than Gene Autry and even had a few big

record hits but never received a big buildup or a large following.

Thunder

Several horses played Thunder, the black stallion in the Red Ryder series. Ryder was played by Don Barry, Wild Bill Elliot, Jim Bannon, and Allan "Rocky" Lane. The Thunder ridden by Elliot was trained by Ralph McCutcheon. Red Ryder was a comic strip hero before he became a movie hero, thus the horse that played Thunder was perhaps at a disadvantage. It was difficult for a real horse to be the equal of the heroic horse drawn by the excellent Western cartoonist Fred Harmon.* Harmon also had a black stallion named Thunder that he rode in personal appearances.

Toby

Toby was the bay horse ridden by Zane Grey's King of the Royal Mounted.

White Eagle

Buck Jones used Silver in most of his movies, but before he obtained him, he used a white horse named White Eagle. Perhaps White Eagle was so named because he appeared in *The Flying Horseman* (1926). Two of his other films were *Branded Sombrero* (1926) and *Cowboy and the Countess* (1926).

White Fury

White Fury was one of the horses ridden by Jack Hoxie (*see* Scout). Lefty Flynn co-starred with a horse called White Fury in the serial *Golden Stallion* (1927).

THE "NO-NAME" STARS

Several Western stars had horses that were not readily identified by the public. Men such as

Audie Murphy, Dale Robertson, and Ben Johnson appeared in many Westerns, but their horses were not given elaborate parts. Nevertheless, horses were an important contribution to their success. The following is a brief discussion of the movie mounts of five of the greatest western stars—Randolph Scott, Joel McCrea, John Wayne, James Stewart, and Gary Cooper.

Randolph Scott

Randolph Scott started making movies in the thirties. He made many films adapted from Zane Grey novels and appeared in a wide variety of roles in the forties. In the fifties and sixties he devoted his time strictly to Western roles. His image was that of the strong loner with strict rules. He rode many horses during his more than thirty years of movie-making. One of his favorites was Steel from the Fat Jones Stable.

Randolph Scott starred in many movies based on Zane Grey novels.

*Thunder wasn't the only comic strip horse to make the movies. Sparkplug of the Barney Google strip was "brought to life" in movies such as *Hillbilly Blitzkrieg* (1942). Silver of the Lone Ranger series was also a comic-strip horse. Many of the movie horses—Trigger, Champion, Topper, Koko,—were featured in comic books after they were successful in the movies.

John Wayne as Rooster Cogburn with Dollar.

sociated with Westerns to win an Oscar.* He has directed and produced Westerns. Yes, John Wayne has done it all.

Wayne did not come to Hollywood as an experienced cowboy as did other stars such as Buck Jones. He had on-the-job training. He credits much of his riding ability and expertise in stunts, such as falling from running horses, to the training he received from Yakima Canutt. He was willing to learn from the more experienced cowboys. Dana Serra Cary in *The Hollywood Posse,* which was primarily a biography of her father, a cowboy extra, wrote, "John Wayne was universally respected and liked by the cowboys—unlike many of the stars."

Wayne has ridden many different horses throughout his long, illustrious movie career. Many of his early movies were done with limited funds and limited numbers of horses. One article stated that in one movie the budget was so tight that they couldn't afford more than one horse, so in the first scene, Wayne knocked out the heavy and stole his horse (which had been stolen from the heroine's brother). One of

*Gary Cooper won an Oscar for *High Noon* (1952). Warner Baxter won one for his portrayal of the Cisco Kid in *In Old Arizona* (1928), and Lee Marvin got one for *Cat Ballou* (1965). Walter Brennan won three Oscars for supporting roles in *Come and Get It* (1935), *Kentucky* (1937), and *The Westerner* (1940). Other winners of Oscars for supporting roles were Thomas Mitchell (*Stagecoach*, 1938) and Burl Ives (*The Big Country,* 1958). Ben Johnson, long a star of Western movies, won one for his supporting role in *The Last Picture Show* (1971), a movie about a small Texas town in the 1950s. The only Western movie to be awarded an Oscar for best picture was *Cimarron* (1931). *In Old Arizona* (1929), *The Ox Bow Incident* (1942), *High Noon* (1952), *The Alamo* (1960), and *Butch Cassiday and the Sundance Kid* (1969) were nominated but did not win.

59

the first horses he rode in pictures was a little buckskin from Arizona. Wayne said, "Lucky for me, he was not a skittery horse. When we worked in Montana on the buffalo range, most of the horses took a dim view of charging into the baffalo herd and caused many a rider to stake claims here and there over that range."

When Wayne was asked the name of the white horse he rode in many of early movies he replied, "For six pictures, I did have one white horse that they named after me—Duke. But the majority of the horses that appeared to be white that you saw me ride were gray, dapple gray, light palomino, or white or whatever happened to be available on whatever location we were on. We weren't spending enough money on the pictures to afford a lead horse." The six movies John Wayne made with Duke were *Ride Him Cowboy* (1932), *The Big Sampede* (1932),

Haunted Gold (1933), *Telegraph Trail* (1933), *Somewhere in Sonora* (1933), and *Man From Monterey* (1933). In answer to the question of which was his favorite horse, Wayne said, "My favorite horse that I rode in the fifties and sixties was a big bay named Banner. He was not a purebreed, but he was intelligent and had an instinct for our business; and as you know, horses have likes and dislikes. He loved me and disliked a hellava lot of other people." Wayne also frequently rode a horse named Henry in the 1950s and 60s. Both animals were owned by the Fat Jones Stables. Even though Wayne was particularly fond of Banner and tried to buy him, Jones wouldn't sell. Thus, Banner was used by other cowboy actors. For example, Bob Steele was also fond of Banner and tried to use him whenever possible.

Wayne spoke one of the most interesting lines

James Stewart on Pie and with Dean Martin and Raquel Welch in *Bandolero!* (1968).

any movie cowboy ever said to his horse. In *True Grit* (1969), as Rooster Cogburn, he lay pinned under his horse that had been shot and said, "Dammit Bo, First time ya ever gave me reason to curse ya." The horse in *True Grit* was played by a Quarter Horse called Dollar. According to some reports, Wayne wasn't happy with Dollar at first but he grew to appreciate him. In fact he used Dollar in the sequel to *True Grit, Rooster Cogburn* (1975).

James Stewart

James Stewart began his cowboy career at a later age than most of the big Western stars. He starred in the Western satire *Destry Rides Again* in 1939 with Marlene Dietrich, but his Western career really started with *Winchester, '73* in 1950. The movie was a success and he quickly became considered as a Western star. *The New York Herald Tribune* wrote, "Stewart takes to horses and fast shooting as though he had been doing nothing else throughout his illustrious career." Some of his other Western movies were *Broken Arrow* (1950), *Bend of the River* (1952), *The Naked Spur* (1953), *The Man Who Shot Liberty Valance* (1961), *The Man From Laramie* (1955), *The Rare Breed* (1966), and *Firecreek* (1967).

Stewart's favorite horse was an impressive chestnut gelding named Pie. *The New York Times* when reviewing *The Far Country* (1955) wrote, ". . . astride an arch-necked majestic stallion, which Stewart sits and rides well, he is an impressive figure." The critic should be forgiven for calling Pie a stallion. It is part of the Hollywood myth that all he-man cowboys ride stallions. In fact most of the "stallions" were geldings. Pie was a part Thoroughbred owned by Steve Meyers. Stewart tried to buy Pie but Meyers refused to sell, thus Pie was use by other Western stars such as Audie Murphy. Pie was ridden first by Stewart in *Winchester '73* in 1950. He continued to appear in Stewart's movies until he was retired at the age of twenty-nine after the filming of *Bandolero* in 1968. Stewart also had a radio show called "The Six Shooter," and his script horse was named Scar.

Gary Cooper and one of his early favorite horses.

Gary Cooper with the big black horse in *Springfield Rifle* (1952).

Gary Cooper

Gary Cooper was the epitome of Western stars for many moviegoers. His strong, silent characterizations delighted millions of fans. He appeared at home on a horse and, in fact, did spend some time on a Montana ranch during his youth. Many fans might be surprised to learn that Cooper also co-starred with a horse. In *Arizona Bound* (1927) and *The Last Outlaw* (1927) he shared billing with Flash, "The Wonder Horse." Cooper rode many different horses during his career. The horse with the most striking markings ever ridden by Cooper was probably the animal he rode in *Nevada* (1927), *Wolf Song* (1929), and *Fighting Caravans*

(1931). The horse was a chestnut with four white stockings, an almost completely white face, and a watcheye. Tyrone Power rode the same horse in *Jesse James* (1939), indicating that that particular horse had a long career.

Another interesting horse was the gray named Pete ridden by Cooper in *The Westerner* (1940). Judge Roy Bean (Walter Brennan) wrongly accused him of stealing the horse and arrested him. Cooper saved himself from hanging by talking about Lily Langtry, whom the Judge worshiped. Cooper was another one of the stars who liked Fat Jones's Steel. He rode him in *It's a Big Country* (1951). Cooper's most famous Western movie is probably *High Noon* (1952), but he really had little to do with horses in that movie except for the shoot-out in the livery stable.

One of the most attractive horses ridden by Cooper was a black stallion in *Springfield Rifle* (1952). Lon Chaney, Jr. tried unsuccessfully to ride the stallion and abused the horse when he failed. Cooper rescued the horse from Chaney and, of course, rode him without difficulty.

3
The Versatile Stars

Of course there have been many equine stars in addition to those that appeared with the Western stars. Many of them appeared in a wide variety of movies but were seldom given billing. Nevertheless, they were well known by those working in the movie industry.

They were also frequently lauded by the critics, or at least preferred to the human actors. For example, the *Variety* critic wrote, "Texas Dandy [the horse] is about the best thespian in the film," when reviewing *Boy From Indiana* (1950) with Lon McCallister.

Anna

The March 23, 1940 issue of the *New York Times* carried a very interesting obituary. It reported the death of Anna, a horse star of the opera *Aida*. It said that Anna carried tenors for twenty-five years. She died at the age of thirty-nine and was cremated. Prior to her career in opera, she was a movie horse. She carried Rudolph Valentino in *The Sheik* (1921) and Marion Davies in *When Knighthood was in Flower* (1922).

Black Diamond

Black Diamond, a large, black American Saddlebred stallion was owned by the Fat Jones Stable. He appeared in *The Track of the Cat* (1954), *Red Canyon* (1949), *Flame of Araby* (1952), *Black Horse Canyon* (1954), and many other movies during his twenty-year movie career. He won the Craven Award and Awards of Excellence from the Animal Humane Association in 1951 for *Black Midnight* and in 1952 for *Flame of Araby*. Les Hilton said that he was one of the most versatile horses in the business.

Butterfly

Butterfly was one of the animal stars of the Mack Sennett menagerie. He was in a series of comedies in which he did stunts such as jumping off roofs into pools of mud. Butterfly could be called the Soupy Sales of the equine actors.

Diamond Jet

The Fat Jones Stables' current black horse star is a Thoroughbred gelding. Dyke Johnson purchased him for the stable from Dick Crow after Jet had a short career on the race track. Diamond Jet hasn't had as many opportunities to act as Misty and Black Diamond, his black horse star predecessors at the Fat Jones Stable, because there are not as many movies being

Diamond Jet, current black horse stallion star of the Fat Jones Stable.

could do a variety of tricks, but it was his striking coloring that drew attention. Even though Dice was a pinto, it was reported that his sire was an Arab X Thoroughbred cross and his dam was reported to be an American Saddle Horse X Thoroughbred cross. He appeared in many Westerns, including *Duel in the Sun* (1946). Jean Arthur rode him in *Arizona* (1940). Gene Autry rode Dice in a few of his earlier movies. Bill Elliot and Richard Dix also rode him. Dice made *Life Magazine* because of a publicity stunt. *Duel in the Sun* was filmed on location in Arizona. Gregory Peck rode Dice into the dining room of the Hotel Santa Rita. *Life* called Dice "one of Hollywood's finest performing horses." Dice was trained to pull a revolver from a pocket, knock down cowboys, boost cowboys by the seat of the pants, kneel, lie down and play dead, count numbers with a hoof, bow, and smile or yawn upon command. In one picture, Dice went through a hotel lobby, entered an open elevator, decided it was too small, backed out, and climbed the stairs. His last film was *Thunderhoof* (1948), a story of a wild pinto stallion co-starring Preston Foster. He died at the age of thirty.

After Dice retired, McCutcheon replaced him with a pinto named, logically, Domino. This pinto was ridden by Charleton Heston in

produced that require horses. But he has distinguished himself. He starred in *Smoky* (1966) with Fess Parker, *The Reward* (1965) with Max van Sydow, and in a Walt Disney television movie, *The Rascal* (1969) and several other movies. Les Hilton, who worked with many of the great horses such as Misty, Black Diamond, and Mr. Ed, called Diamond Jet one of the most intelligent horses he has ever worked with. Diamond Jet sired a few foals before he was gelded, and one of his sons, Hud, was Paul Newman's mount in *Butch Cassidy and the Sundance Kid* (1969), and Ryan O'Neal's in *The Wild Rovers* (1971).

Dice

Ralph McCutcheon has trained many horses, such as Fury and King Cotton. His first successful horse was a pinto stallion named Dice. Dice

Jean Arthur and Dice in *Arizona* (1940).

64

The Big Country (1955) and by Rory Calhoun in his television series "The Texan."

Flicka

A star of his own television series, Flicka also had movie experience. One report claimed Flicka replaced another chestnut gelding as the lead in *Tonka* (1958). About halfway through the filming of *Tonka* the lead gelding simply got tired of working and wouldn't respond. Flicka was brought in, painted to look like the gelding, and finished the movie in great style. Flicka, an Arabian, was trained by Les Hilton. The "Flicka" series was another example of Hollywood's style. Flicka, supposedly a mare, was played by a gelding.

Fury

This black American Saddle Horse stallion from Missouri was also trained by Ralph McCutcheon. One of his first roles was in the Twentieth-Century Fox production of *Black Beauty* (1946). Another important role was in MGM's *Gypsy Colt* (1954), for which he was awarded a Patsy. He portrayed a wild stallion in *Wild in the Wind* (1957) with Anthony Quinn and was Elizabeth Taylor's horse in *Giant* (1956). He was ridden by Clark Gable in *Lone Star* (1952) and by Joan Crawford in *Johnny Guitar* (1954). However, he was made famous by his television series. He played the lead in "Fury" for five years and at that time was one of the most well-known horses in America. Peter Graves was Fury's human co-star. Graves, the brother of James Arness of "Gunsmoke" fame, went on to a very successful acting career including the popular television series "Mission Impossible." Graves said, "I got a flat salary but the horse [Fury] and his trainer got a bigger salary plus five percent of the show's overall net. But the horse was the real star—without that horse, I wouldn't have made the money I made." In 1958 *Time Magazine* wrote, "*Fury* is not another western . . . packed with each Saturday morning episode is a plain little moral . . . Fury's success is due less to the horse sense it propounds than the exciting horseflesh it displays. No ordinary nag, Fury (real name:

Beauty) is one of the best-trained, best paid horses in Hollywood. He works only four months a year and has brought owner Ralph McCutcheon $500,000 in eight years. His *Fury* fee: $1,500 a show."

King Cotton

One of the most impressive-looking of all movie horses is King Cotton, a large, white majestic animal. He is one-quarter Arabian, one-quarter Morgan, and one-half American Saddle Horse. He was trained by Ralph McCutcheon. He was ridden by Charleton Heston in *Diamond Head* (1962), by Sara Lane in "The Virginian" television series, by Cantinflas in *Pepe* (1960), and by Peter Ustinov in *Viva Max* (1969). He won the Craven Award in 1957 and a Patsy for his work in *Pepe*.

Little Buck

A buckskin with white blaze and white stockings, he has many credits. He was used by Robert Horton in the television series "Wagon Train" and "Man From Shenadoah," and by Doug McClure in "The Virginian." Trained by Del Combs, he was also used as a stunt horse and won the Craven Award in 1965.

Mister Ed

This palomino was star of the television series (1961–64) about a talking horse. He was born in 1954 and given the name Bamboo Harvester. The series was really a takeoff on *Francis, The Talking Mule*. Alan Young played the bumbling owner, Les Hilton trained the horse, and Arthur Lubin was the director. Alan "Rocky" Lane supplied the voice.

Misty

One of the most famous performers was a black Thoroughbred named Missed-A-Shot or Misty, owned by the Fat Jones Stable. He was retired from the race track because of a bowed tendon. He was particularly good as a fighting stallion, but unlike Rex was a gentle horse and quite easy to work with. He was a race horse in

The Gentlemen From Dixie (1941). He played the stallion Banner in *My Friend Flicka* (1943) and *Thunderhead, Son of Flicka* (1945). He fought Gregory Peck in *Duel in the Sun* (1946).

His career lasted twenty-five years, and Fat Jones claimed that Misty was his favorite all-time movie horse.

Old Baldy

Several movie horses were named Old Baldy because of their bald faces. One such Old Baldy, trained by Buster Trow, was an excellent rearing horse and won the Craven Award in 1959. The current Old Baldy in the Fat Jones Stable is the favorite horse of several actors. He is a gentle, dependable horse that has enough action to make the rider look good but is no threat to the inexperienced rider. He appeared

on the television version of "The Skin Game" with Larry Hagman, and he was ridden by Slim Pickens in *Blazing Saddles* (1974).

Old Fooler

The present star of the Fat Jones Stable is Old Fooler. A very distinctive roan horse with a white blaze, he has appeared in many movies. Perhaps his greatest achievement was in *The Rounders* (1965), where he got the best of Glenn Ford and Henry Fonda. He appeared in the television series based on *The Rounders* and in *The Scalp Hunters* (1968) with Burt Lancaster. When Ossie Davis tried to ride away with Old Fooler, Lancaster whistled and the horse stopped and threw Davis.* He had a large role as H-Bomb in *Flap* (1973), where, among other stunts, he got drunk. His co-stars in *Flap* were

*Burt Lancaster played the same trick on Virginia Mayo in *The Flame and the Arrow* (1950) but with a different horse.

Slim Pickens on Old Baldy in *Blazing Saddles* (1974).

4
Characteristics of Movie Horses

The kind of horse is important. The screen hero is not likely to ride just any old pony. He is going to be partly identified by his horse. Roy Rogers' palomino or the Lone Ranger's Silver could be spotted miles away on the screen so one knew that rescue was at hand even without the surge in the music.
—J. Calder, *There Must Be a Long Ranger.*

COLORS

For many situations, solid-color horses were preferred by the movie directors. Bays, blacks, and chestnuts were the most prevelant selections. Horses with distinctive markings, such as an odd-shaped blaze or irregular spots, were not liked by producers. If the color was too striking, it was feared that the audience's attention would be captured by the horse and that they would watch him instead of the actor. Distinctive markings also made it more difficult to use doubles. Another reason to use solid colors was that many horses were versatile and were used to playing several different parts in the same movie. In one scene, a horse might be used to pull a buggy, but perhaps in subsequent scenes he would have to pull a plow, herd cattle, or pull a stagecoach, all for different owners. A solid-color horse made it difficult for the viewer to recognize him as playing several parts.

The white horse has long been emblematic of victory and associated with power, pride, and glory. St. George is usually depicted on a white horse. Many artists have painted leaders such as Napoleon and George Washington astride white horses.

Thus, it was natural that the Western hero, at least in the B movies, frequently rode a white horse. White horses were also very effective in black and white movies, since they provided a good contrast. It was also easy for the audience to identify the hero in chase scenes when he rode a white horse. In contrast, the villain seldom, if ever, rode a white horse in the B movies. Not all cowboy stars had white horses but enough did that it was frequently stated that the good guy could always be identified because he wore a white hat and rode a white horse.

Many of the white horses were really grays that had lightened in color with age. Famous white horses included the Silvers of Buck Jones, the Lone Ranger, and Sunset Carson, Tex Ritter's White Flash, John Wayne's Duke, Hopalong Cassady's Topper, Charles (The Durango Kid) Starrett's Raider, Jack Perrin's

Advertisement for *Down Texas Way* (1942).

Starlight, Fred Thomson's Silver King, and Whip Wilson's Silver Bullet. John King, Reb Russell, Tim McCoy, Bob Livingston, and Buster Crabbe also rode white horses in most of their movies. George Houston rode a white horse in the Lone Rider series, perhaps to help identify with Lone Ranger series. Richard Boone had two gray horses, Curly and Frisco, in his "Have Gun, Will Travel" series. He alternated the grays with two bays—Rudy and Mexico.

Pintos and paints were used much less frequently than solid-color horses as lead horses. As mentioned earlier, it was much more difficult to get a double for a spotted horse than for one of solid color. Nevertheless, several pintos were used. The most famous of course, was William S. Hart's Fritz. Jimmy Wakely and David O'Brien also rode pintos. O'Brien starred in *Phantom Pinto* (1941) and *Pinto Bandit* (1944). Tonto's Scout, Duncan (Cisco Kid) Renaldo's Diablo, and Little Beaver's Papoose were pintos. Roy Stewart rode a pinto named Ranger. Bob Barker rode a pinto named Apache. Bill Patton rode a pinto in "The Pinto Kid" series. Lee Powell rode a pinto in *Trigger Pals* (1939) and Raymond Hatton rode a pinto in the "Rough Riders" series with Buck Jones and Tim McCoy. A beautiful pinto was the co-star of the television movie *Peter Lundy and The Medicine Hat Stallion* (1977).

Michael Landon as Little Joe rode a pinto horse named Cochise in the early episodes of "Bonanza." However, in September 1964, Cochise was so badly mutilated by vandals that he had to be destroyed. His pinto replacement was named Concho. It was reported that Concho was sold to John DuPont of Pennsylvania for ten thousand dollars at an auction sale at the Fat Jones Stable after the "Bonanza" series was completed.

Monte Montana rode his trick pinto Rex in many public appearances and in movies such as *The Man Who Shot Liberty Valance* (1962). Dorothy Page, the "Singing Cowgirl," rode a pinto in movies such as *Water Rustlers* (1939).

James Drury rode an Appaloosa in "The Virginian" television series.

ger and Tarzan, but many other palominos were also stars. Jack Luden rode a palomino in his movies filmed in the late twenties and early thirties. Hoot Gibson rode palominos such as Mutt, Goldie, and Pride of Oregon in several of his movies. Johnny Mack Brown rode a palomino named Rebel. Eddie Dean had Copper and Tim Holt had Lightning. Leo Carrillo as Pancho rode a palomino in "The Cisco Kid" series. Carrillo also raised palominos on his ranch in southern California. Rod Cameron had Knight. Kermit Maynard, Ken's brother, also road a palomino. Stewart Granger favored palominos. He rode one named Wagonmaster in the "Man From Shiloh" television series. It was also reported that, at one time, he owned a horse called Gold Coast that was subsequently used in the "Mr. Ed" television series. Russell Hayden often rode palominos. John Wayne

Holy Smoke in *Run Appaloosa Run* (1966).

One of the most attractive movie horses: the palomino ridden by Cleavon Little in *Blazing Saddles* (1974).

rode one in *War Wagon* (1967), Errol Flynn rode one in *Montana* (1950). One of the most beautiful palominos ever to appear in movies was the one ridden by Cleavon Little in *Blazing Saddles* (1974).

Roans were not commonly ridden by the hero. Even in the filming of *The Strawberry Roan* with Ken Maynard in 1933 and Gene Autry in 1948, a roan was not used. Maynard used Tarzan and Autry used Champion. Autry's movie was in technicolor. Thus, it required a good deal of imagination on the part of the audience to accept the chestnut Champion as the strawberry roan. John Wayne rode a roan in *The Big Trail* and Tom Mix used a roan, Old Blue, prior to his acquisition of Tony. Gary Cooper rode a roan named Henry Henshaw in *Along Comes Jones* (1945).

Several horse stars were solid color with distinctive white markings. The white markings could relatively easily be duplicated on the double. Tony was a chestnut with a stripe and snip on the face and two white stockings on the rear feet. Tony Jr. was also a chestnut but with four white stockings. Champion was also a chestnut with white stockings. In fact, some people credit Champion's early success to his resemblance to Tony. Steel was another chestnut with white stockings. Joel McCrea's Dollar was a chestnut with a bald face. Bald doesn't mean he didn't have hair, it just means the white on the face included the area around the eyes and nostrils or portions thereof. One of the most attractive chestnuts in movies was the one ridden by Alan Ladd in *Shane*.

Buckskins have a reputation of being tough and possessing a good deal of "cow sense." Thus, it was reasonable that they would be used in cowboy movies. But they seldom were used as a lead horse. Jim Arness had several different Buckskins named Buck or Marshall on his "Gunsmoke" television series, and Lorne Greene used a buckskin on the "Bonanza" series. When the "Bonanza" series was cancel-

Buck, one of the buckskins ridden by James Arness in the "Gunsmoke" series. He was from the Fat Jones Stable.

Roans were not often used by the heroes in B Westerns. But in the real West, roans such as the one above were quite evident and had a reputation for being tough and good cow horses.

John Wayne rode a buckskin in *The Cowboys* (1972).

led, the Fat Jones Stable gave the buckskin to Greene. John Wayne rode a buckskin in *The Cowboys* (1972).

Color was not a major concern in several cases because it could be changed. For example, the producers wanted a horse with a particular conformation and temperament to play Don Quixote's Rozinante in a filming of the Cervantes classic for television. They finally found just the right horse but he was the wrong color. No problem—they just had him painted the correct color every day.

BREEDS

Horses of many breeds—Arabians, Tennessee Walkers, Quarter Horses, Thoroughbreds, American Saddle Horses, Standardbreds, Morgans—have been used as movie horses. Johnny Agee, the trainer of horses such as Tarzan and Champion said, "Western horses need certain characteristics, a long tail, a long mane, an arched neck and the ability to make kids love 'em. These characteristics are chiefly a matter of personality and may show up in any breed." Dyke Johnson of the Fat Jones Stable says that he never considers breed when selecting movie horses. The first priority is temperament. He adds, however, that Quarter Horses are the predominant animals because they look good in Western movies and usually have a more gentle disposition. Philip Rutherford of the Randall Ranch says, "Quarter horses are the best all around horse for the business. Arabians are very pretty and intelligent but many of them are too small and too high strung. Another reason for not using Arabians is that there were very few of them in the Old West."

Bill Elliot claimed that in the forties most Western stars preferred Quarter Horses and rode them whenever possible. Of course, Elliot might be considered slightly prejudiced, since he owned a Quarter Horse ranch. Several other stars such as Dale Robertson, Audie Murphy, and John Wayne also raised Quarter Horses. Robertson rode one of his own Quarter Horses, named Leo, Jr. in his "Tales of Wells Fargo" series. Leo Jr. was of good Quarter Horse breeding. His sire was the famous Leo and his dam was a Zantonan mare.

The Morgan breed has had several outstanding individuals used in the movies. The breed is characterized by attractive horses with short backed bodies, proud, arching necks, and imposing style. They often move with a lot of action. Rex, the "King of the Wild Horses," was reported to be a Morgan. KoKo, Rex Allen's horse, was one-half Morgan. I think the photographs of the original Tony indicate that it is more likely that he had Morgan blood rather than Percheron, as was indicated by some of the press releases. King Cotton, although a white horse, was claimed to be one-quarter Morgan. Several other Morgans, such as Blackman Allen (appeared in *Courage of Black Beauty,* 1957), were also used in the movies. Morgans such as Heritage Allen and Burckland Pride starred in *Justin Morgan Had a Horse* (1965).

The Morgan breed developed from one stallion, Justin Morgan, who was an early New England horse (1789–1821). The breed was and is still primarily based in New England, but it was used by many Northern Cavalry Troopers in the Civil War. After the war, many individuals of the breed were taken out West where they were highly prized. Thus, the use of Morgan Horses in Western movies is just as authentic as the use of Quarter Horses.

In 1940, Tim Holt spent a good deal of time looking for a movie horse and said he wanted a Thoroughbred X Morgan cross, but he finally decided on an individual that was an American Saddle Horse. American Saddle Horses are similar to Morgans in that they are stylish and majestic. The are slightly larger and a bit more streamlined than Morgans. They are noted for a beautiful head carried on a long, graceful neck, high-set tail, and proud action. Representatives of the American Saddle Horse breed include Tim Holt's Duke (a registered animal), Ken Maynard's Tarzan (one half Saddle Horse), Black Diamond, Dice (one-quarter Saddle Horse), Fury, and King Cotton (one-half Saddle Horse). Rex, the big black horse ridden by Lloyd Bridges in the midsixties in the television series "The Loner," was a registered American Saddle Horse with the name of Montrose Sea. Rex also had the lead in the *Fighting Stallion* (1950) with Bill Edwards.

The Tennessee Walking Horse is similar to the American Saddlebred Horse but is generally heavier, more powerful, and coarser. The breed

Ken (Roddy McDowell) and his mother (Rita Johnson) discuss Thunderhead's racing career in *Thunderhead, Son of Flicka* (1948).

though the above examples are colorful, they wouldn't be appropriate for a movie star—particularly a Western star.

The origin of the name was also important in the movies and the name was frequently explained. Flicka was suggested as the name for the filly by Gus, the farmhand, because it means "little girl" in Swedish. Thunderhead, "The Son of Flicka," was named Goblin when he was young but when he won his first practice race,

Ken's mother said he deserved a better name. She said, "Thunderheads! They are like white horses in the sky. Let's call him Thunderhead." Clint Barkley explained that he named his horse Smoky because, "Where there is smoke there is fire and he has plenty of fire. His father was a proud wild stallion." Several wild stallions were called Wildfire because they were fast and uncontrolled.

In *Peter Lundy and the Medicine Hat Stallion* (1977) Peter named his horse Domingo because Peter had read that the first horses had landed in North America in 1493 at Santo Domingo.

5
The Livery Stables

Several stables specialized in renting horses to the movie studios. One of the most well-known suppliers is the Fat Jones Stable. Clarence "Fat" Jones was born in Rome, New York, in 1893, but his parents moved to Los Angeles in 1905. Jones started in the livestock business as a teenager. He bought a pair of burros to pull a grocery delivery cart. He traded the burros for a buckskin named Chick and soon bought another one named Buck. In 1912 he sold the horses to a Pathé film unit and his career was started. His first really big assignment was to supply eleven hundred horses for the filming of *Cimarron* in the late twenties. Over the years the Jones Stable has had many of the versatile star horses. There was Diamond Jet, Black Diamond, Steel, Crown Prince, Misty, Old Fooler, Old Baldy, Blanco, and Sunny Jim, to name a few. In the fifties and sixties the stables supplied horses for the many television Western. Some of the horses supplied were Don Durant's Bingo in the "Johnny Ringo" series, Hugh O'Brien's Candy in "Wyatt Earp," and Guy Madison's Buckshot and Andy Devine's Joker of the "Wild Bill Hickok" series. In 1962 the Fat Jones Stable was purchased by Dyke Johnson. The stable has changed locations sev-

eral times as the Los Angeles metropolis has grown. From the present location in Devonshire Downs it continues to be one of the most popular stables. With the decreased production of Western movies in Hollywood in recent years, the television shows such as "The Cowboys," "Kung Fu," "Dirty Sally," and "Gunsmoke" have been among the stable's biggest clients.

The largest stable of the 1970s is the Randall Ranch in Newhall, California. Two of Glenn Randall's sons, Corky and J. R., train horses

Old Fooler giving Dyke Johnson of the Fat Jones Stable a friendly push.

80

Three pictures of Jadaan illustrating the change from grey to white with age. The top picture shows him and Rudolph Valentino in *The Son of the Sheik* (1926). The middle picture is as he was ridden by Victor McLaughlin in the 1929 Rose Parade. The bottom picture (Jadaan on the right) was taken in 1931.

Will Rogers rode the Arabian, Letan, in *The Texas Steer* (1927).

Donald O'Connor as a jockey in *Sing You Sinners* (1947).

Cojo Rojo, the star of *The Appaloosa* (1966).

ridden by Will Rogers in *Texas Steer* (1927).

The four "Arabian" stallions (Atair, Rigel, Antares, and Aldebaran) driven by Charleton Heston in *Ben Hur* were Lippizans imported to Rome.

One of the largest groups of horses ever assembled for movies was for *Undefeated* (1969) with John Wayne and Rock Hudson. In the film John Wayne gathers a herd of twenty-five hundred horses to take south of the border to sell them. The movie was filmed near Durango, Mexico. The horses were rented from several Mexican villages. It took about four weeks to assemble the horses and brand them with a hot iron on the hoof so that they could be returned to the correct village. It took about two weeks to return them after the filming was over. Thus, the collection and return took almost as long as the actual filming. During the filming, they moved the twenty-five hundred horses a total of eighteen miles. At one point, the horses were strung out for six miles. The wranglers were rightly proud of the fact that less than a dozen of the twenty-five hundred horses failed to be returned to the villages.

Marlon Brando's co-star in *The Appaloosa* (1966) was taken from the racing circuit to audition for the part. The producers of *The Appaloosa* had been searching for several months for just the right horse and looked at hundreds of horses before selecting Cojo Rojo. He was owned by Jack and Sylvia Martinez of the Centurion Ranch of Saugus, California. As the editors of the *Appaloosa News* said, "That Cojo Rojo could come from the race track where horses are keyed up to a razor's edge and turn in the magnificent performance that he did in *The Appaloosa* is a credit to both Cojo Rojo and the Appaloosa breed." Cojo Rojo's work was increased because Black Mountain King, one of his Appaloosa doubles, died of cancer during the filming and Bobby Davenport had to teach King's stunts to Cojo Rojo.

In many of the racehorse movies, the real McCoys were used. For example in *The Gentleman Rider* (1919) with Violet Hopson and Stewart Rome, the racehorse Ghurke played the part of Jupiter. Donald O'Connor rode Bing Crosby's racehorse Ligarote in *Sing You Sinners* (1947). Ligarote was a very successful horse. In fact he almost beat Seabiscuit in a match race at the Del Mar track. The horse in the Disney television movie *Ol' Hacksaw* (1958) was the Thoroughbred Siren Prince by Hill Prince and out of Royal Siren from the Leslie Combs III Spendthrift Farms. Glenn Randall trained him for the Disney studio.

Many horses are bought on location. For example, when *Ivanhoe* (1951) was filmed in England, Yakima Canutt, the action director, reported that he was able to buy all of the horses he needed from English farmers for an average of $210. When the filming was over, he sold them for a profit.

Several of the early Westerns were filmed on the Millers Brothers 101 Ranch in Collings, Oklahoma. For example, *North of 36* (1924), *On With the Show* (1926), and *Trail Dust* (1927) were filmed at the ranch and the studios rented the ranch horses and hired the cowboys.

6
Movies about Horses

Numerous movies have been made about horses. It is beyond the realm of this book to describe or even list all of them. However, it might be interesting to reminisce about several of them. *Flicka* (1943) starred Preston Foster (Rob) as the ranch owner and Roddy McDowell (Ken) as his son. Flicka's mother, Rocket, was a very fast horse but rather unmanageable. Foster sold her, but as she was leaving the farm she was killed when she leapt from the truck and hit her head. Foster said that her foal would be loco, too, and wanted to get rid of it, since "a loco horse isn't worth the bullet it takes to shoot it." McDowell was attracted to the foal and was determined to train it. After many difficulties, such as Flicka's running into a barbed-wire fence,* and becoming severely wounded and being almost killed by a mountain lion, Flicka proved to be a good horse, and McDowell and Foster developed a better father-son relationship. The producers of Flicka tried to film the movie without hiring trained horses. They had so much difficulty that they finally realized they would save a lot of money if they brought in Jack Lindell and some trained animals.

*The fence was really made of rubberbands painted to look like wire.

Thunderhead, Son of Flicka (1948) was also made with animals trained by Jack Lindell. Lindell worked for the Fat Jones Stable and is generally considered the greatest horse trainer in the history of Hollywood. Blanco and nine other horses from the Jones Stable played Thunderhead. In this sequel to Flicka, Roddy McDowell (Ken) bred Flicka to the neighbor's Thoroughbred racing stallion. He wanted to get a racehorse in order to save the Goose Bar Ranch from financial ruin. The result of the mating was the white horse, Thunderhead.* Thunderhead proved difficult to handle because he was a throwback to the Albino, his grandsire on the maternal side. The Albino was a wild stallion that raided mares from the ranchers. Thunderhead was fast but unpredictable. In his first race he appeared to have it won easily, but he bolted off the track. He not only lost the race but suffered a bowed tendon, which prevented him from ever racing again. Things looked bad for the Goose Bar Ranch because few mares were left and the Albino killed Banner, the Goose Bar Ranch Stallion. But Thunderhead saved the

*Unfortunately, according to the present understanding of horse genetics, it would be impossible to obtain a white horse from the mating of two solid colored horses even if a grandparent were white.

88

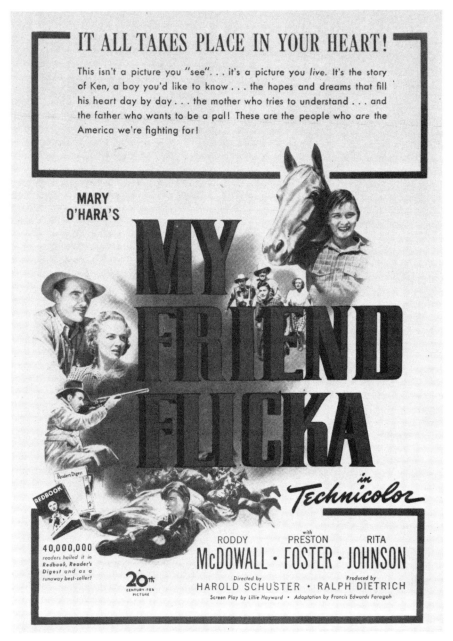

Advertisement for *My Friend Flicka* (1943).

ranch. He led the way to the secret canyon where the Albino kept the stolen mares. Thunderhead killed the Albino in an exciting fight and drove the herd back to the ranch. Ken freed Thunderhead because he was now the "King of the Stallions."

Black Beauty, Anna Sewell's novel to protest the abuse of horses, has been the basis for several films. One of the first was *Your Obedient Servant*, filmed in 1917. It was released in 1921 and retitled *Black Beauty*. Another silent version of Black Beauty was released in 1921 by Vitagraph. It starred Jean Paige and James Morrison. Other versions included one released in 1933 with Alexander Kirkland and Esther Ralston and one released in 1946 starring Mona Freeman and Richard Denning. In 1946 Black Beauty was played by Highland Dale. *The New York Times* critic wrote, "Horses are wonderful actors and the one in this picture is no exception."

Black Beauty (1971) with Mark Lester and

89

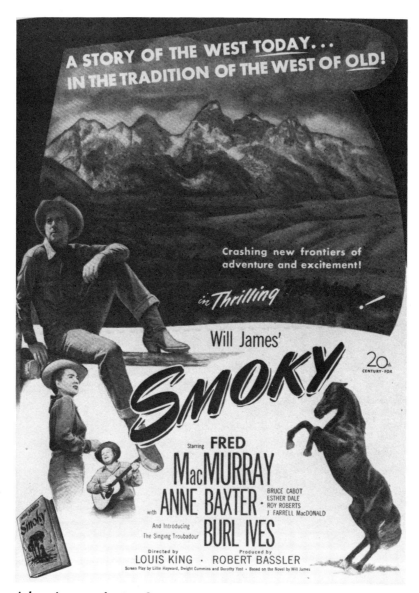

Advertisement for *Smoky* (1946).

Walter Slezak was an English production. *The Courage of Black Beauty* (1957) was not based on Sewell's novel. At least one television series was called *"Black Beauty."*

Will James's classic story about *Smoky, The Cow Pony* has also been filmed several times. Victor Jory was in the 1933 production and Rex, *"The Wonder Horse,"* played the part of Smoky. In 1946 Country Gentleman played Smoky in a movie starring Fred MacMurray, Ann Baxter, and Burl Ives. Diamond Jet played Smoky in 1966 and Fess Parker played his cowboy friend. Smoky was a wild horse captured by cowboy Clint Barkley. Barkley was betrayed by another cowhand, and Smoky was sold to the rodeo, but eventually Barkley and Smoky were reunited and returned to the ranch.

Another Will James horse story, *Sand*, was filmed in 1949 with Mark Stevens, Rory Calhoun, and Coleen Gray. *Sand* was the story of a pampered show horse who escaped into the wilds after a train accident and turned wild. Jubilee played the lead. *Variety* wrote, "Sand has an agreeable cast who support the magnificent equine hero of the tale." Mark Stevens played the wealthy horse owner and Rory Calhoun was a ranch foreman who hated Jubilee because the stallion was the cause of the death of Rory's mare.

John Steinbeck's *The Red Pony* was filmed in

Anne Baxter, Burl Ives, and Bruce Cabot watched Fred MacMurray tame the wild stallion in *Smoky* (1946).

1949 with Robert Mitchum. One critic summarized the plot as follows: "Experiencing grief and despair over the death of his pony, a young boy loses faith in those he loves until the birth of a colt brings him an understanding of life."

A horse of another color, a palomino was the star of a movie of that name in 1949. Jerome Courtland rescued Beverly Tyler's prize stallion that had been stolen by Roy Roberts. One reviewer wrote, ". . . interest is particularly sharpened by the beauty and antics of a young palomino colt." The lead was played by a horse named California, and he won a Patsy for his efforts.

Still another color, *Indian Paint* (1966), told of the story of a fifteen-year-old Indian boy's attempt to raise and train a paint colt. The colt was the offspring of the tribe's finest mare and a great white wild stallion. One reviewer wrote, "The boy and colt became separated from the tribe and it is many moons before they return home, both have achieved a special maturity and understanding." The film won the *Parents'*

Magazine Family Medal Award. The stars were Johnny Crawford, Robert Crawford, Jr., and Jay Silverheels.

Gallant Bess (1947) starred Marshall Thompson with Silvernip as Gallant Bess. Silvernip's trainer was Joe Atkinson. Silvernip's acting was fine and Bess was billed by the studio as "the horse with a human mind." Thompson played a Seabee in the South Pacific. He wanted to get a leave to visit his mare, which was about to foal. He got his leave only after a long delay, and his mare died before he could see her. However, he returned to duty and found another mare on a Pacific Island, trained her, and they all lived happily ever after.

Misty (1961) told the story of the ponies of Chincoteague. A mare named the Phantom was captured by two children. The mare had a foal named Misty. The children decided that it was not fair to keep the ponies from being free, so they released them. The Phantom returned to the Chincoteague Island, but Misty returned to the children.

Snowfire (1958) was about a little girl and a wild white stallion. The girl claimed that the

Many movies, such as *Red Stallion* (1949), featured
fights between horses and other wild animals.

stallion could talk to her. The ranchers want to capture the stallion but the girl helped him escape and hid him. But when the girl was injured in a fall, Snowfire helped rescue her by attracting the attention of the hunters.

Two Thoroughbreds (1940) was the story of the love of an orphan boy for a homeless colt.

In *Wild Beauty* (1946) a young Indian boy saved the life of a young colt but eventually let him go back to his wild herd.

In *The Red Stallion* (1949) young Ted Donaldson loved the stallion but he knew that

in order to save the ranch he had to sell Red for a big price. Ted trained Red to be a racehorse, and it appeared that Red was ready to be a champion when he encountered the bear that killed his mother. Things looked grim but the horse defeated the bear, won a race, and Ted got to keep the ranch and Red.

In *Run Wild, Run Free* (1970) ten-year-old Philip Ransome (played by Mark Lester) had been incapable of speech since birth. His only friends were a young girl (Fiona Fullerton) and retired Colonel (John Mills). The movie ads stated, "The lives of all three are deeply affected when they encounter a magnificent wild white colt with pale blue eyes. A new and inspiring world of love and communication opens up for Philip as a result of his experiences with the beautiful white horse."

Gypsy Colt (1954), with Donna Corcoran, Ward Bond, Frances Dee and Fury, was an equine remake of *Lassie Come Home* (1943). It was the story of a girl's pet horse that the father had to sell to a racing stable. Gypsy broke away from the stable and traveled five hundred miles to return home.

Then one hallo, boys, one loud cheering hallo!
To the swiftest of coursers, the gallant, the true
For the sportsman unborn shall the memory bless
Of the horse of the highwayman, bonny Black
    Bess.*

Dick Turpin was a highwayman in England in the early 1700s. He and his black mare, Black Bess, were immortalized by W. H. Ainsworth in his book *Rookwood* in 1865. Ainsworth said that Black Bess was a magnificent horse with striking beauty, perfect conformation, and great endurance. Her sire was reported to be a desert Arabian and her dam was a coal-black English racer. According to the legend, Turpin rode Black Bess from London to York in one night, a feat never before accomplished, in order to establish an alibi and to escape capture. The story of Turpin and Black Bess was filmed several times. The British and Colonial Kinematograph Co. produced *The Adventures of Dick Turpin* (1912) and *Dick Turpin and the Death of Bonnie Bess* (1913). *Dick Turpin's Ride to York* (1922) starred Matheson Lang. Tom Mix played Dick Turpin in 1925.

Louis Hayward starred in *The Lady and the Bandit* in 1951 and David Weston played the lead in *The Legend of Young Dick Turpin* in 1965. The real Dick Turpin was not nearly as noble as the Turpin of the screen. He was hanged as a horse thief in 1739 at the age of thirty-three. He had a horse named Black Bess, but the story about the ride to York was fiction.

*From *Rookwood* by W. H. Ainsworth.

MUSTANGS OF THE MOVIES

Movies about wild stallions or mustangs have long been popular. It is easy to see why mustang movies capture an audience's attention. Mustangs are unique animals. J. Frank Dobie wrote, "Halted in animated expectancy or running in abandoned freedom, the mustang was the most beautiful, the most spirited and the most inspiring creature ever to print foot on the grass of America."

Jenni Calder wrote, ". . . The indomitable stallion, the most splendid symbol of freedom. The symbolic value of the horse is immense, whether it is the rearing untamed stallion at the beginning of the *Hombre* (1967) or the Lone Ranger's Silver."

Of course, it is paradoxical that the mustang or the wild stallion—the symbol of freedom—in the movies is always captured and tamed. Mustangs were also captured in real life but, unfortunately, only a small percentage of the captured mustangs developed into first-class horses. Most were of poor quality and were difficult to train. It was estimated that one of every three mustangs died before the animals were trained. Hence, in reality, many mustangs were hunted for dog meat rather than to be captured and trained. Many were killed by ranchers because the mustangs ate grass that the ranchers wanted for cattle. But in the movies, the captured mustangs became champions.

The movie cowboy often captured the stallion by rescuing him, the stallion and cowboy became loyal friends, and then the stallion rescued the cowboy. For example, Tony portrayed a wild mustang in *Just Tony* (1922). Tom Mix rescued him from being beaten by a cruel ranch-hand. Later, Tony returned the favor by saving not only Tom but also Tom's girlfriend, the ranch owner's daughter. A similar story was told in *My Pal* (1925) with Dick Hatton and Star and in *Phantom of the Desert* (1930) with Jack Perrin and Starlight. Of course, there were some minor variations to the theme. Rex, the "King of the Wild Horses," portrayed a horse called Black Cyclone in a movie of the same name in 1925. He was rescued from quicksand by Guinn (Big Boy) Williams. Rex then saved the mare Lady from a pack of wolves and rescued Williams not only from outlaws but also from a mountain lion. Rex still had enough energy to defeat Killer, a stallion that was trying to corral Rex's band of mares. In *King of the Wild Horses* (1934) Rex was saved by Red Wolf, an Indian boy. Together they defeated the villain, who had fake papers authorizing him to kill sick and infected horses. Instead, he was rounding up all the Navajos' horses (sick or not) and killing them for their hides.

In *Wild Beauty* (1927) the captured stallion Thunderhoof, played by Rex, won a race and defeated the villains, thereby enabling Hugh Allan to pay off the mortgage of his California ranch and marry his cowgirl sweetheart. White Star, one of Rex's competitors, was cast as the wild stallion King, in *King of the Herd* (1927). He bested the bad guys by winning the Santa Barbara polo matches and the Travor Cup. *Wild Fire* (1945) starred Bob Steele, Eddie Dean, and

Sterling Holloway. The stallion Wild Fire was accused of rustling horses. The ranchers hunted him and managed to wound him, but Steele saved him. When Wild Fire's wound was healed Steele released him, but the grateful stallion returned to help Steele capture the rustlers. *The Adventures of Gallant Bess* (1948) was billed as a story about the loyalty of a wild mare to the cowboy who captured and trained her. The cowboy was played by Cameron Mitchell.

Many other examples can be given. John Wayne saved Duke, a white stallion, in *Ride Him Cowboy* (1932). Jack Beutel saved a wild stallion that was ordered to be killed in *Mustang* (1952). Preston Foster rescued Thunderhoof in *King of the Wild Horses* (1949). In fact, almost every Western star and many stars not normally associated with Westerns appeared in a movie about wild horses.

Gene Autry was a wild-horse wrangler in *The Old West* (1951), and he captured a wild stallion

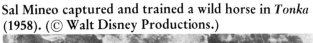

Sal Mineo captured and trained a wild horse in *Tonka* (1958). (© Walt Disney Productions.)

in *Comin' Round the Mountain* (1936). Charles Starrett rounded up a herd of wild horses to help an Indian orphan in *Cyclone Fury* (1951). Monte Hale hunted for an outlaw stallion in *Man From Rainbow Valley* (1946). Hoot Gibson caught and tamed a wild mare in *Hurricane Kid* (1925). Joel McCrea pursued a wild stallion in *Cattle Drive* (1951) and in *Mustang Country* (1976). He captured and tamed a horse in *Black Horse Canyon* (1954) and won the hand of the lady ranchowner. Audie Murphy captured an entire herd of wild horses in *Sierra* (1950). Rory Calhoun caught mustangs in *Apache Uprising* (1966). Don Murray caught a wild horse, Sugar, in *These Thousand Hills* (1959). John Gilbert tamed a wild horse by whistling in *The Lone Gambler* (1948) and cleared the stallion of a murder charge. Clark Gable chased wild horses in his last movie, *The Misfits* (1961). Sonny Tufts captured a wild stallion and a wild bull in *Untamed Breed*. Roddy McDowell tamed a wild horse in *Black Midnight* (1949) and Sal Mineo did the same in *Tonka* (1958). The Mesquiteers (Bob Livingston, Ray Corrigan and Max Terhune) rounded up wild horses in *Riders of the Black Hills* (1938).

Many of the Zane Grey novels were made into movies. Grey's novels were highly romantic and frequently featured horses. Wildfire was filmed as *When Romance Rides* (1922) and *Red Canyon* (1949).

In *The Lion and the Horse* (1952) Steve Cochran and his partners capture a seal-brown stallion (Wildfire), but before Cochran could raise the money to buy out his partners, they sold the horse to a rodeo owner (Ray Teal). Wildfire became a bucking star, and the owner refused to sell him to Cochran. Cochran freed Wildfire and then recaptured and trained him. Teal tried to take the horse back, but Wildfire killed him. However, the horse was pardoned and returned to Cochran after he killed an escaped lion that had been terrorizing the countryside.

The outlaws wanted to poach wild horses from a wild horse reservation in *Hit the Saddle* (1937). They painted a killer stallion (Volcano) to look like the pinto leader of the wild horse herd. Volcano had been trained to kill when he heard a shrill whistle. The outlaws had Volcano kill the sheriff so that they could blame the wild-horse leader and justify capturing the horses. The Three Mesquiteers (Robert Livingston, Ray Corrigan, and Max Terhune) suspected foul play. They captured the real stallion, and Stoney (Robert Livingston) easily tamed him. They discovered that the sheriff was killed by a horse wearing horseshoes, but of course the wild pinto didn't wear shoes.

The outlaws captured Stoney and commanded Volcano to kill him. But the wild pinto, tamed by Stoney, came to his rescue and drove off Volcano. Stoney's friends arrived and the two outlaws jumped on Volcano in an attempt to escape, but when Stoney whistled, Volcano trampled the outlaws.

Several wild-horse movies were based on Zane Grey novels. Grey's novel *Wildfire, The Story of a Wild Horse* was filmed as *When Romance Rides* (1922) with Claire Adams and Carl Gantvoort and as *Red Canyon* (1949) with Howard Duff and George Brent. The movies *Wildfire* (1925), with Aileen Pringle, and *Wild Fire* (1945), with Bob Steele, were not based on Grey's novel of the same name, nor did the two movies have the same plot. The 1925 movie was about a racehorse. Grey's *Lightning* (1927) was filmed starring Jobyna Ralston and Robert Frazer. *Wild Horse Mesa* was filmed three times, in 1925 with Jack Holt and Noah Beery, in 1932 with Randolph Scott, and in 1947 with Tim Holt (Jack Holt's son). *Heritage of the*

Desert was filmed in 1924 with Ernest Torrence, 1932 with Randolph Scott, and 1939 with Donald Woods. It was claimed that the wild stallion Silvermane in *Heritage of the Desert* was based on White King, a real-life horse pursued without success by Zane Grey and Buffalo Jones in Arizona.

Wild horses were also captured in the Arabian deserts. Jeff Chandler tamed a wild stallion (played by Black Diamond) and raced him to victory to save Araby and win Princess Maureen O'Hara in *Flame of Araby* (1951). As Miss O'Hara said, "There is no steed in all of Araby that can outrun the mighty black stallion."

Other wild-horse movies or serials included *Devil Horse* (1932) with Harry Carey and Frankie Darro, *Wild Horse Stampede* (1932) with Rex, *Wild Mustang* (1936) with Harry Carey, *Wild Horse* (1931) with Hoot Gibson, *Wild Horse Stampede* (1943) with Hoot Gibson, Ken Maynard, and Bob Baker (The Trail Blazers), *Wild Horse Roundup* (1936) with

Zane Grey, a dentist from Ohio who became the most prolific writer of Western novels. The novels were panned by the critics but achieved great popularity.

96

producers must have wondered, too, because they made many race movies during the next sixty years.

The use of color increased the effectiveness of race movies. When writing about *The Home-stretch* (1947) the reviewer from *Motion Picture Herald* wrote, ". . . the story serves merely as a framework for exciting race shots. But there are few other subjects which the technicolor camera can record better than the turbulent commotion of the racing crowd, the smart costumes, the excited prancing of well-groomed horses and the thrilling course of the race itself."

A popular theme was horse wins race and saves family fortune and farm. But the racehorse usually had to overcome adversity, and his trainer or jockey was usually trying to make a comeback or make amends for earlier mistakes. For example, Al Jolson played Gus, a trainer in *Big Boy* (1930). The horseowner's children didn't have much faith in Gus or in Big Boy, and they tried to convince their father to get rid of them. Crooks tried to steal the horse, but Gus and Big Boy prevailed, won the race, and restored faith in their ability.

The manner in which the horse was spurred on to victory was often quite ingenious although usually not realistic. In *No Control* (1927) a circus horse was entered in a race. The jockey knew that the horse was afraid of lions, and roared like a lion in the horse's ear and scared him to victory. Max Davidson won a race with a horse called Dynamite when he whispered Yiddish into the horse's ear. A similar trick was used on the mare Sarah in *Pleasure Before Business* (1927). In *Blue Blood* (1950), (Tanglefoot) starring Bill Williams and Arthur Shields, an old Thoroughbred is saved from becoming dog food and made into a winner when it was found that the horse's only problem was that he was afraid of the starter's red flag (the scriptwriter obviously did not realize that horses cannot distinguish between colors). The villain tried to frighten the horse by having a jockey wear red silks.

A group of cabdrivers bought a horse in *The Day the Bookies Wept* (1939). The horse was a loser until he drank a barrel of beer. Joe Penner played the trainer.

In *Racing Blood* (1954) Mr. Marker was spurred on by the whistle of his young friend,

Jimmy Boyd. Rory Calhoun fixed a Sunday, non-betting race so that a worn-out trotter could win one more time in *County Fair* (1950). The stewards and other owners were all in on the plan so that the old fellow could retire gracefully after a final victory. In *Riding High* (1949) a crooked jockey tried to hold back Broadway Bill but Bill took the bit from the jockey and managed to win. However, he worked so hard he "broke" his heart and died on the track.

In *Money from Home* (1953) with Dean Martin and Jerry Lewis, Lewis was racing against a crooked jockey in a steeplechase. Both jockeys were knocked off their horses and the crooked jockey by mistake mounted Lewis's horse, My Sheba. Lewis cut across the field, jumped on the horse, both men rode My Sheba across the finish line, and My Sheba was declared the winner.

Music was also used to inspire horses to victory. In *David Harum* (1934) with Will Rogers, an old plug named Cupid was turned into a champion by the power of music. Seems he ran fast whenever he heard ta-ra-ra-ra-bum-de-aye. Herbert Munder played a cabbie who purchased an ex-cavalry horse in *Call It Luck* (1934). The horse went from last to first when Munder played "Charge" on the bugle. Misty Summer won a race in the television series "San Pedro Beach Bums" because he hated "Yankee Doodle." The trainer told the jockey to sing "Yankee Doodle" in the horse's ear. "He hates that song and will do anything to get away from it." The race was almost lost when the jockey forgot the tune of "Yankee Doodle."

Lon McCallister was a jockey in *The Boy From Indiana* (1950). He worked for a trainer (George Cleveland) who gave aspirin to the horses so that they would win. The jockey, the trainer, and Groucho Marx all gave "vitamin" pills to Little Shamrock in *A Girl in Every Port* (1952) and the horse set a track record. A racoon inspired a horse to victory over a Stanley Steamer in *Rascal* (1969).

Another method of winning the race was to simply convince the horse that he could win. In *National Velvet* (1945) Mickey Rooney asked Elizabeth Taylor how she thought she could possibly win the Grand National with her horse, Pie. Her answer was, "By knowing that the Pie can win and telling him so." She also said, "He'll be an enchanted horse with invisible wings to take me over every jump." In *Francis Goes to the Races* (1951) a filly won a $100,000 race and saved the farm after psychoanalysis by Francis the mule gave the filly her confidence. Lon McCallister convinced both the horse and the trainer, Walter Brennan, that they could win in *Home in Indiana* (1944).

The Reivers (1969) was not a movie about racehorses, but it contained an excellent racing sequence and another unusual way to win a race. Kent Hollingsworth, the editor of *Blood Horse,* a journal of Thoroughbred horses, claimed that the race sequence in *The Reivers* was one of the most exciting Thoroughbred races ever filmed. The story took place in the early 1900s. Steve McQueen, Rupert Crosse, and young Mitch Vogel appropriated the boss's new car for a trip to Memphis while the boss was out of town. In a moment of misguided judgment, Rupert traded the car for a racehorse named Lightning. The only way to recover the car was for the horse to win a race. Unfortunately, the horse was not inclined to run. Rupert discovered that Lightning was crazy about sardines. When spurred on by the smell, Lightning won the race. The action and the photography of the race was outstanding. Roy Barcroft, the veteran of many Westerns, was the race judge. Food also inspired a Thoroughbred named My Girl in *Crazy Over Horses* (1951). The Bowery Boys promised her a banana split if she won. She won the photo finish by sticking out her tongue.

In one of the most amusing movies about races (*A Day at The Races*, 1937), Hi Hat won the race after Harpo Marx, the jockey, showed him a picture of a man whom they both hated in order to convince the horse to run faster.

In many movies such as *Checkers* (1919), *Race Wild* (1926), *Million Dollar Handicap* (1925), *Racing Blood* (1926), *Chain Lightning* (1922), *Thundering Hoofs* (1922), *They're Off* (1922), *Old Kentucky* (1936), and *Women First* (1924), a girl disguised herself as a boy and rode the horse to victory. The most famous such deception was by Elizabeth Taylor in *National Velvet* (1945). Her horse, which was named the Pie, was played by a horse named King Charles. King Charles's previous movie specialty was

Elizabeth Taylor and King Charles from *National Velvet* (1945).

jumping over autos filled with people. The name "Pie" really did not make sense in the movie because King Charles was a chestnut. However, in the book, the Pie was short for *piebald*, an English term for black-and-white horses. The Pie was discriminated against in the book because of the piebald color. Incidentally, Elizabeth Taylor in her youth was quite interested in horses. She even supposedly wrote an article, "Riding a Live Hobby," for *Holiday Magazine* in 1946. The article gave basic advice on how to ride horses, and Miss Taylor said that she had been riding horses since the age of three. She often disdained the use of a double in scenes with horses—sometimes to her regret. A horse stepped on her foot and broke some bones during the filming of *Lassie Come Home* (1943) and she suffered a concussion during the filming of *National Velvet*. It was also claimed that some of the back trouble she experienced in later years stemmed from injuries received while jumping horses as a youngster.

International Velvet (1978), starring Tatum O'Neal, is billed as a continuation of *National Velvet*. It is the story of the romance of a young girl on the British three-day event team and a young boy on the U.S. team. In preparation for the film, Miss O'Neal took riding lessons from Mrs. Marcia Williams. Mrs. Williams has trained many riders and has worked with Walt Disney Studios in movies such as *The Horse With the Flying Tail*. Bill Steinkraus, one of the leading equestrian experts in the U.S., was also hired as a consultant.

Margaret O'Brien (Clara Belle) fell in love

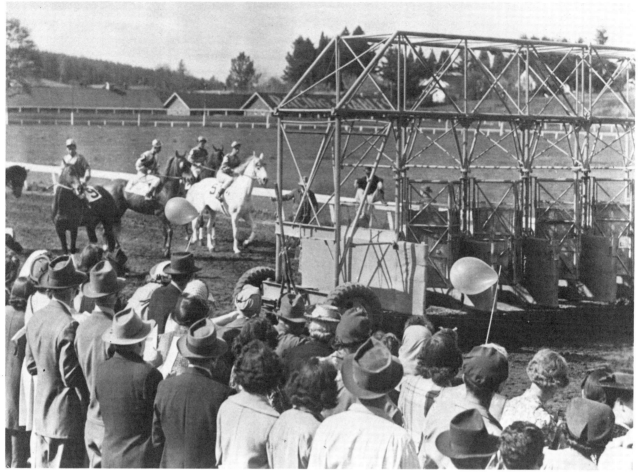

Getting Thunderhead in the starting gate in *Thunderhead, Son of Flicka* (1948).

with a racehorse in *Glory* (1956). Glory won the Kentucky Derby during a thunderstorm. Clara Belle explained, "She was born during a storm and thunder makes her run." (The best part of the movie was the introduction, in which real Thoroughbred champions were shown.)

Not all race movies had gimmicks that enabled the horses to win. The reviewer from *Motion Picture Herald* wrote, "*Ride Kelly Ride* (1941) represents horse racing as horse racing should be—a business." The stars were Eugene Pallette and Marvin Stephens.

Also, the hero's horse didn't always win. In *Green Grass of Wyoming* (1948), Thunderhead, the wild stallion and son of Flicka, ran off with a young mare owned by Robert Arthur. The mare was recaptured and entered into a trotting race against a horse owned by the father of the girl Arthur loves. The father did not particularly like Arthur. It looked as though the mare was going to win the race and the father would think

even less of Arthur when the mare suddenly collapsed. It was discovered that she was healthy but in foal to Thunderhead. In the meantime Arthur had gained the approval of the girl's father.

The horse also lost in *The Fighting Chance* (1955) in a bit of a surprise ending. Rod Cameron and Ben Cooper played a trainer-jockey team. The team was split when they both fell in love with a scheming Julie London and Cameron married London. The team was reunited when they bought Miss Ellen, a fast horse but one that could be handled only by Cooper. The jockey wasn't licensed to train so he had to get Cameron's help. Cooper and Miss Ellen had a chance to win the big race, but Cooper pulled the mare up when she started bleeding from her nose. Miss London showed her true colors when she berated Cooper for pulling up the mare. This made Cameron realize that Miss London lacked character. He left Miss London, and Cooper, Cameron, and Miss Ellen lived happily ever after.

One of the largest jockeys was William Bendix. He and Groucho Marx rode identical twin horses in *A Girl in Every Port* (1952). The horses finished in a dead heat but both were disqualified when it was found that only one twin had been entered and the judges could not tell which was which.

Cornell Wilde married Maureen O'Hara in *Homestretch* (1947). She wanted him to settle down but he wanted to follow the horses. They separated but were reunited when her horse beat his in the big race.

Another familiar theme involving racehorses is one in which a child or naive adult has a knack for picking winners, such as in *The Rocking Horse Winner* (1950) with John Mills and Valerie Hobson, *She Went to the Races* (1945) with Francis Gifford, James Craig, and Ava Gardner, *Three Men on a Horse* (1936) with Frank McHugh, Sam Levene, and Joan Blondell, or *Dear Brigette* (1965) with James Stewart, Glynis Johns, and Billy Mumy. Young Butch Jenkins simply asked the horses who would win in *My Brother Talks to Horses* (1946).

The jockey or trainer turning crooked and then repenting and winning the race was also a reliable theme. One of the best of this type was the film of Hemingway's *Under My Skin* (1950) with John Garfield.

The Rainbow Jacket (1954) had colorful racetrack sequences that sparked the story of how Bill Owen, a veteran jockey gone wrong, repented and taught Fella Edmonds to race properly. Wesley Barry was tempted by a girl and was bribed to lose in *The Thoroughbred* (1930). However, he changed his mind and won the race. Richard Walling was a repentent jockey in *Silks and Saddles* (1929). Jane Chapman salvaged racetrack gambler John Litel in *Little Miss Thoroughbred* (1938).

Winning a race not only saved the farm but sometimes a marriage. In *The Bride Wore Boots* (1946) Barbara Stanwyck loved horses but her husband, Robert Cummings, did not have any use for them. Their squabbles over horses led to a divorce. However, Cummings saw the error of his ways, salvaged an old nag named Albert, rode him to victory in a cup race, and regained the love of the fair Barbara.

According to Ella Smith, Cummings related that the race sequence took thirteen takes. He said, "After each take the man from the Society for the Prevention of Cruelty to Animals would take over and see to it that the horses were cooled down properly and given a rest, and that twelve fresh mounts were saddled up. Markings such as white blazes on the horse's nose were painted on for matching purposes with noninjurious S.P.C.A. approved water color so it would look as though I was always riding the same horse."

Miss Stanwyck was no stranger to horses. She appeared in many Western movies, such as *Annie Oakley* (1935) with Preston Foster, *The Maverick Queen* (1956) with Barry Sullivan, *Cattle Queen of Montana* (1954) with Ronald Reagan, *The Moonlighter* (1953) with Fred MacMurray, *The Furies* (1950) with Gilbert Roland, and *Trooper Hook* (1957) with Joel McCrea. She was also the star of the long-running television Western series "Big Valley." Ella Smith wrote, "She [Miss Stanwyck] has courage, her riding is fast and purposeful, and it is apparent that the medium of the western which she loves so well, is one which she can make a unique contribution."

Barbara Stanwyck and Brian Donlevy in *The Great Man's Lady* (1942).

staged a comeback with a broken-down horse that he rehabilitated. Stanley Clements and Gloria Henry, as brother and sister, inherited two racehorses in yet another movie entitled *Racing Luck* (1948). After one of the horses was claimed in a race by David Bruce, it was discovered that neither horse would run without his former stablemate. It was decided to put both horses in a race—the owner of the winner to get both horses. Miss Henry's horse won and she also won Mr. Bruce. Miss Henry made many movies with horses such as *Sport of Kings* (1947), *Strawberry Roan* (1948) with Gene Autry, *Lightning Guns* (1950) with Charles Starret and Smiley Burnette, *Riders in the Sky* (1949) with Gene Autry, and *Al Jennings of Oklahoma* (1951) with Dan Duryea.

Barry Fitzgerald was a horseplayer in *Easy Come, Easy Go*, (1947) (Elvis Presley played a frogman in a movie with the same name in 1967).

John Ford filmed several racing sequences. In *Kentucky Pride* (1925), Henry Walthall was ruined financially because his mare injured her leg and lost the race. However, her foal, named Confederacy, grew up and won a big race, enabling Henry to buy back the mare, which had been sold to a livery stable. *The Shamrock Handicap* (1926) starred Janet Gaynor and told the story of an Irish horse that came to America to win the $25,000 Shamrock Handicap in order to save the farm in Ireland. John Wayne's first part in a Ford film was as a spectator at the racetrack in *Hangman's House* (1928). Wayne's only part was to smash a picket fence during the excitement of the race. There was an exciting race sequence in Ford's *The Quiet Man* (1952), which starred John Wayne.

In *Stablemates* (1938) Wallace Beery was a disbarred veterinary surgeon who had taken to excessive drinking. Mickey Rooney was a young jockey who decided to help Beery. He restored Beery's self-respect and won a race with a horse that had been cured after an operation performed by the reformed Beery.

Basil Radford was a retired major who owned a pet shop but wanted to own a racehorse in *Galloping Major* (1950). He formed a syndicate of three hundred people to buy the mare, Montana Miss, but somehow ended up with a gelding of questionable ability named Father's Folly. The horse could not run on the flat track,

so the syndicate named him Galloping Major and entered him in the Grand National Steeplechase. at Aintree. Radford, although considerably overweight, had to substitute for the jockey at the last minute, but justice prevailed in what the steward called "the most incredible race I've ever seen."

Randolph Scott and Jackie Coogan as brother owners of a racing stable had to fight gangsters who were determined to fix a race in *Home on the Range* (1935). Ann Sheridan provided the love interest. Scott and Coogan weren't the only ones who had to fight crime at the racetrack. Warner Oland also did so in *Charlie Chan at the Racetrack* (1936), and Hugh Beaumont as Michael Shayne had to trap a gang that was counterfeiting winning pari-mutuel tickets in *Too Many Winners* (1947). Jack Hedley as an insurance investigator broke up a gang that fixed races in *Never Back Losers* (1967). *Breezing Home* (1937) starred William Gargan and Binnie Barnes and was about crooked bookies.

John Payne rode the horse Cavalier to victory in a cup race in *Maryland* (1940) after Walter Brennan came to his aid. Mickey Rooney was an egotistical jockey with a horse named Pookah, and Judy Garland as Cricket West added some songs in *Thoroughbreds Don't Cry* (1937). Rooney was also a jockey in *Down the Stretch* (1963). He had to overcome his father's unsavory racing record.

Two Dollar Better (1951) told the story of a businessman, played by Jon Letel, who developed racetrack fever and could not stop betting. Marie Windsor played the feminine lead. Women got the betting fever in *The Gambling Sex* (1932) with Ruth Hall and Grant Withers.

A racehorse saved a church by winning a race in order that the mortgage could be paid off in *Father Tom* (1921). Van Heflin won a horse race to get material to build a church in *Count Three and Pray* (1955). An Indian boy trained a horse to win money for a village shrine in *For Love of Mike* (1960). The stars were Armando Silvestre, Richard Basehart, and Arthur Shields. Several Mexican boys won $81,513 when they combined their money with a dime taken from the church poorbox and placed a lucky bet in *Dime with a Halo* (1963). Unfortunately, they lost the ticket before they could collect the winnings.

Many comedians appeared in racehorse movies. If the idea of Harpo Marx as a jockey sounds a bit ridiculous (*A Day at The Races*, 1937), think of *Crazy Over Horses* (1951) in which Huntz Hall of the Bowery Boys played a jockey, or think of Percy Kilbride driving a trotting horse in *Ma and Pa Kettle at the Fair* (1952). Leo Gorcey of the Bowery Boys rode a racehorse, Sweet Alice, to help an elderly stable owner in *Muggs Rides Again* (1945). Stu Erwin was a trainer in *Great Mike* (1944). Abbott and Costello had Teabiscuit in *It Ain't Hay* (1943). They stole the horse by mistake but disguised him by putting sun glasses on him. The Hoosier Hot Shots helped a trotting horse win in *Arkansas Swings* (1948). The Ritz Brothers had a racehorse in *Straight, Place and Show* (1938) and the Dead End Kids had one in *That Gang of Mine* (1940). The idea of a "bunch of kids" helping an old-timer win a race was repeated in many movies and television shows. One of the most recent filmings was in an episode of "San Pedro Beach Bums." One of the "bums" took over when the jockey got hurt and he rode the horse to victory.

Horserace movies about Kentucky, the home of the Thoroughbred racing industry, are plentiful. Examples are *Kentucky Derby* (1922) with Reginald Denny, *Kentucky Handicap* (1926) with Reed Howes, *Kentucky Pride* (1925) with Henry Walthall, *My Old Kentucky Home* (1922) with Monte Blis, *A Song of Kentucky* (1929) with Joseph Wagstaff, *Bred in Old Kentucky* (1926) with Viola Dana, *Blue Grass of Kentucky* (1944) with Bill Williams, *Old Kentucky* (1936) with Will Rogers, *Pride of the Bluegrass* (1939), and *Blue Grass of Kentucky* (1956) (Blue Grass was the name of the horse). Concerning *The Lady's From Kentucky* (1929) with George Raft, Ellen Drew, and Zasu Pitts, one critic wrote, "Regardless of the title, Raft's horse takes precedence over his lady in the usual but well done horseracing saga."

Many movies contained racing scenes. One of the first Technicolor movies produced in England—*Wings of the Morning* (1937)—starred Henry Fonda and had a crucial horse-race scene. *Saratoga Trunk* (1945) with Gary Cooper and Ingrid Bergman had racing scenes at Saratoga Springs.

Although no horses were shown, a race was an important part of *The Sting* (1973), in which Paul Newman and Robert Redford conned a big racketeer out of a million dollars by using a fake bookie joint. A long racetrack robbery sequence was an important part of the movie *The Killing* (1956), with Sterling Hayden and Vince Edwards. *The Sundowners* (1960), with Robert Mitchum and Deborah Kerr, had an interesting race scene. The horse named "The Sundowner" appeared to have won the big race but was disqualified for interference. Mitchum really was not too unhappy. If the horse had won, he would have to had settled down.

One of the most exciting film races was the chariot race in *Ben-Hur* (1959). Yakima Canutt planned and directed it. Charleton Heston played Ben-Hur and Stephen Boyd played Messala. The exciting race with all the wrecks and turnovers was reportedly filmed without any serious injuries to man or horse—a tribute to Canutt's stunting and planning skill. Heston claimed that he drove his own chariot through eighty-five percent of the race. In an interview with Pete Martin for the *Saturday Evening Post*, Heston said, "I started driving it two months after the shooting began and I did it almost everyday until gradually I learned how. I couldn't drive it well but that wasn't necessary. All I had to do was learn to stay on board so they could film me there. Once I'd learned to drive, even badly, MGM could guarantee that I would win." The race was only on the screen for eleven minutes, but it took several weeks of preparation and several days of filming.

The filming of *Ben-Hur* in 1925 also had the exciting race, but reports indicate that two horses were killed and several men severely injured. To ensure a fast race, the producer gave a prize of $250 to the winning driver. In the 1925 production, the Roman Imperial Guard was portrayed by the members of Troop B Eleventh Cavalry from the Presidio at Monterey, California. The horses were of uniform height and all dark bays and added greatly to the beauty of the picture.

One of the longest races on film was the seven hundred-mile endurance race in *Bite the Bullet* (1975). The reviewer for *Films in Review* wrote that the movie was "a paean to horses."

One of my favorite racing scenes was in *Friendly Persuasion* (1956). Gary Cooper

Barry Fitzgerald discusses the Thoroughbred problem in *The Story of Seabiscuit* (1949).

Horses were used in many action movies, such as
Sword of Lancelot (1963) starring Cornel Wilde.

Hollywood horses in the Hollywood hills pretend they
are Roman horses.

Soldiers from *Cleopatra* (1943).

Afghanistan lord's stablemaster. Horses were an important ingredient in many Errol Flynn non-Western swashbuckers, such as *Adventures of Don Juan* (1948), *Adventures of Robin Hood* (1938), and *The Charge of the Light Brigade* (1936).

Horses were ridden in many movies with Canadian settings, particularly in movies about the Mounted Police. Pierre Berton claimed that Hollywood greatly misrepresented the Canadian west, and the role of the horses was no exception. Berton wrote, "Horses were ridden under the most improbable conditions in Mountie movies—over the tops of mountains, through jungle-like forests, off the edges of cliffs and, of course, through the eternal snows of the Great Woods." Hollywood was also very clever when titling the Mountie movies or serials. Examples are *McKenna of the Mounted* (1932) with Buck Jones, *Clancy of the Mounted* (1933) with Tom Tyler, *O'Malley of the Mounted* (1921) with William S. Hart, *Moran of the Mounted* (1926) with Reed Howe, *Glenister of the Mounted* (1926) with Lefty Flynn, *Steele of the Royal Mounted* (1925) with Bert Lytell, *McGuire of the Mounted* (1923) with William Desmond, and *Law of the Mounted* (1929) with Bob Custer. Other Mountie movies included *North West Mounted Police* (1940) with Preston Foster and Gary Cooper, *Pony Soldier* (1953) with Tyrone Power, and *The Wild North* (1951) with Wendell Corey and Stewart Granger.

Tyrone Power rode horses effectively in *King of the Khyber Rifles* (1953) and *Captain From Castile* (1947). He rode the beautiful Arabian Barakul in *Suez* (1938). Cornell Wilde was a dashing horseman in movies such as *Bandit of Sherwood Forest* (1946), *Sword of Lancelot* (1963), and *At Sword's Point* (1952). Jon Hall portrayed a horseman from the Middle East in *Arabian Nights* (1942) and *Ali Baba and the Forty Thieves* (1943).

The cavalry of the British Empire were portrayed in many movies. Examples are Flynn's *The Charge of the Light Brigade* (1937), *Khartoum* (1966) with Charleton Heston, *Lives of a Bengal Lancer* (1935) with Gary Cooper, *Khyber Patrol* (1954) with Richard Egan, and *Zulu* (1964) with Stanley Baker.

English horsemen from an earlier age were portrayed in *Ivanhoe* (1952), *Knights of the Round Table* (1953) with Robert Taylor, *Black Arrow* (1948) with Louis Hayward, and in many more. One might assume a horse also had an important part in *Lady Godiva* (1955) with Maureen O'Hara and in *Lady Godiva Rides Again* (1957).

In *Africa Texas Style* (1967) Hugh O'Brien took Quarter Horses to Africa to help capture wild animals. Another aspect of horses was used in *Quackser Fortune Has a Cousin in the Bronx* (1970) with Gene Wilder. Quackser Fortune (Gene Wilder) follows horses around Dublin collecting manure and selling it for gardening. One day the horses are banished and are replaced by cars, and Quackser is out of a job. Fortunately, a rich cousin in the Bronx dies and leaves an inheritance enabling Quackser to marry the beautiful American exchange student.

Apes rode horses in the *Planet of the Apes* series. The horse in *The Godfather* (1972) will readily be remembered by anyone who saw the movie. The most unusual horse role was in *You Never Can Tell* (1951), in which Joyce Holden was a humanimal horse. Dick Powell was a dog. Horses have appeared in so many movies of so many different types that it would be almost impossible to name a star who hasn't appeared in a movie with a horse. Greta Garbo rode a horse in *The Painted Veil* (1934). Humphrey Bogart was an Irish stablemaster in *Dark Victory* (1939). Rita Hayworth, Carole Lombard, Joan Crawford, Larraine Day, Marge Champion, Jane Wyatt, Barbara Bel Geddes, Jennifer Jones, Gene Tierny, Ann Baxter, Joan Bennett,

World War I scene from King Vidor's *The Big Parade*
(1925) starring John Gilbert.

Robert Taylor, shown here in *Savage Pampas* (1967),
was one of the matinee idols who turned primarily to
Westerns and action movies in the later stages of his
career.

Gregory Peck and Burl Ives in *The Big Country* (1958).

THE LOVE OF HORSES

I compare you my love to a mare of Pharoah's Chariots.—"Song of Solomon," Chap. 1, Verse 9.

Julie London, Evelyn Keyes, and Elke Summer are examples of famous actresses who appeared in Westerns early in their careers. On the other hand, many male stars such as Robert Taylor turned to Westerns late in their career. Mary Pickford's last movie, *Secrets* (1933), was a Western. Shirley Temple kept a pony at the orphanage in *Curly Top* (1935).

Horses were often used symbolically in movie. titles. There was *Behold a Pale Horse* (1964), *Ride on a Dead Horse* (1962), *Dark Horse* (1932), *Four Horsemen of the Apocalypse* (1921 and 1962), *Horse Feathers* (1932), *Horse for Horse* (1940), *Horse's Mouth* (1958), *The Green Mare's Nest* (1965), *They Shoot Horses Don't They* (1969), *Hold Your Horses* (1920), *Horseplay* (1934), *Horse Laugh* (1920), *Sea Horses* (1926), and *Double Harness* (1933).

Horses show many emotions, such as anger, fear, curiosity, hate, jealousy, dislike, and affection. As discussed earlier, horses frequently appear to develop affection for other animals, and such relationships are common among Thoroughbreds. War Admiral had a pet rabbit. Fervid had a bantam rooster and both appeared in *Broadway Bill* (1934) in which Fervid played Bill and the rooster played the mascot, Skeeter. Exterminator, the Kentucky Derby winner of 1918, had a pony mascot named Peanuts. When the pony died, the gelding became disturbed and remained so until his owners tested several ponies and finally found one that Exterminator would accept. Papyrus had a black cat and Mad Hatter had a German Shepherd.

116

Silver the dog and Holy Smoke become friends in *Run, Appaloosa, Run* (1966). (© Walt Disney Productions.)

Affection between horses and other animals was depicted in movies such as *The Sad Horse* (1959). David Ladd and his grandfather, played by Chill Wills, were living on a ranch. Patrice Wymore brought her racehorse, North Wind, to the ranch to let him recover from the loss of a dog to which he was greatly attached. North Wind accepted Ladd's dog as a replacement for the dog he lost and was ready to race again. Wymore wanted to take the dog to keep North Wind happy at the track. David didn't want to give up his dog, so he ran away with him. But he decided that he was selfish and returned and gave the dog to Miss Wymore because the horse and dog got along so well together.

Two in Revolt (1936) was the story of a colt and Shepherd dog born on the same day on a Montana ranch. They became close friends but both fled to the wilds. Lightning (the dog) became the leader of a wolf pack and Warrior led a wild herd. Eventually they met and together returned to the ranch. A dog and a horse were close friends in *Run, Appaloosa, Run* (1966).

The affection of horse for man often depicted in movies is greatly exaggerated. In fact, it is doubtful that horses really develop true affection for humans. Margaret Self concluded,

that horses have any real affection for humans of the sort that dogs display, I doubt. That they recognize specific persons and often enjoy their company, that they sometimes show evidence of liking to be handled and stroked, yes. But, I do not believe that they demonstrate the kind of affection that a mare shows toward her foal. . . . The horse shows no signs of being regretful when his owner leaves him nor anything like the loyal devotion of the dog that never wants to leave his master's side.

The basic premise in many Western films that horses would save their owners in emergencies because they love them is false on two counts. First of all, horses enjoy people's company but I don't think they really love people. Secondly, horses are of little use in an emergency that requires quick thinking because their strongest reaction is fear. Their greatest defense is flight. Thus, having a horse enter a burning barn and chew the ropes off a cowboy was nonsense. But it was the kind of nonsense we enjoyed. Furthermore horses are not really intelligent in the ways in which intelligence is measured in man. That is, they can't reason. Fortunately, they are creatures of habit and usually can be readily trained.

Although horse may not love man, there is no doubt that man loves horses. The great affection of mankind for horses is shown in movies such as *Misty, Red Stallion, Flicka, Smokey, National Velvet, Gallant Bess,* and *Black Beauty* in a highly sentimental fashion. In *A Girl in Every Port* (1952) when Don Taylor's fiancee told him "You've got to choose! That horse or me!" Taylor replied "Well it's this way. You can't run as fast as he can." The love of a cowboy for his horse was told repeatedly. Randolph Scott was more concerned with his mare than with gold in the *Walking Hills* (1949). Robert Young was wrongly accused of murder in *Relentless* (1948) and was almost captured when he stayed to help his mare foal rather than make an easy escape. Jack Beutel as Billy the Kid was willing to trade his girl for a strawberry roan stallion in *The Outlaw* (1947). Kirk Douglas played a modern cowboy with old-fashioned ideas in *Lonely Are the Brave* (1962). He thought one of the most important things in life was his horse, Whiskey. He got into trouble with the law but managed to escape with his horse in spite of the jeeps and helicopters of the police. Only an accident stopped him. He and his horse were hit by a truck when they were crossing a highway in the night and the horse had to be shot.

117

Harry Carey was a down-on-his-luck cowboy in *Cheyenne's Pal* (1917). He was forced to sell his horse, Cactus. When he learned that the horse was to be sent to France for use in the war, he got a job on the ship so that he could steal Cactus. He was caught, but the ship's captain was understanding and let Harry keep the horse and work off his debts. Vaughn Monroe sang "A Man's Best Friend Is His Horse" in *Toughest Man in Arizona* (1952). In *Something Big* (1971), when Dean Martin was asked why his horse had gold inlays in his teeth, Dean replied "Because I love my horse." The movie had many other ridiculous lines.

Not all the movie cowboys loved horses. Glenn Ford told tenderfoot Jack Lemmon that cowboys really hated horses in *Cowboy* (1956). Of course, most real cowboys thought highly of their horses. C. H. Long, a Texas cowboy, was quoted by *Life Magazine* as saying, "If it weren't for a good horse, a woman would be the sweetest thing in the world."

Perhaps the best advice was that given to Margaret O'Brien by Walter Brennan in *Glory* (1956): "Never fall in love with just one horse, love 'em all, Not just one."

But it wasn't only cowboys who loved horses. *Thoroughbreds* (1945) was about a cavalry sergeant (Tom Neal) who received a medical discharge at the same time his unit was mechanized and the horses were sold. In order to be near his favorite horse, he took a job on the ranch of the man who bought him. Neal and the horse won a big race and Neal won the rancher's daughter.

Wallace Beery was also an old-time cavalry sergeant in a unit that was being mechanized in *The Bugle Sounds* (1942). He went on a rampage when his favorite horse was killed by a tank that got out of control. Eventually it was found that saboteurs had tampered with the tanks.

Walter Huston played a tough artillery sergeant who had no love for anyone or anything other than the artillary horse that saved his life in World War I in *Keep 'Em Rolling* (1934). After the war the horse was sold by the Army at auction. Huston stole the horse from the new owner but he was caught and court-martialed. When the affection of Huston for the horse was explained, both he and his horse were allowed to remain in the Army. A hansom cab driver became so distraught when his mare, Molly, died that he lost the will to live, but the people of Chinatown bought him another horse and he recovered in *The Year of the Horse* (1966).

Even Russian films portrayed the love of man for horses. In *The Colt* (1961) a Red Army Cavalry soldier found new meaning in life when his mare foaled. He was ordered to kill the foal but instead hid her. When the foal wandered behind enemy lines, the soldier rescued him, but the soldier was mortally wounded. He lived long enough to see foal and mare reunited.

But the horse did not always win, sometimes the girl did. In the final scene of *The Pathfinder* (1953) George Montgomery kissed the girl and his Indian companion, Jay Silverheels said, "Girl much better than horse."

7
Disney's World

The Walt Disney Studios produced many movies about horses. Although Disney was famous for cartoons, few of the Disney films about horses were animated. He used mice, ducks, dogs, chipmunks, bears, and many other animals as cartoon heroes, but seldom used the horse as the main character. Horace Horsecollar never made the big time. But, whenever horses were used in animated features, they were well done. Brom Bones's black stallion, Daredevil, in *Legend of Sleepy Hollow*, (1949) was magnificent. Ichabod Crane's worn-out old mount, Gun Powder, was a near-perfect caricature. Pecos Bill's fiery horse, Widowmaker, was also excellent in *Melody Time* (1948). Widowmaker was jealous of Bill's girl, Slue Foot Sue. She tried to ride Widowmaker but he threw her high into the air and she landed on her bustle. The bustle acted like a metal spring and bounced her higher and higher until she landed on the moon. Poor Bill mourned for his lost love by howling at the moon. The coyotes copied Bill, hence the reason that coyotes bay at the moon is explained.

A Disney cartoon horse that is a favorite of mine is Cyril, the fun-loving horse that accompanies J. Thaddeus Toad on his adventures in *The Wind in the Willows* (1949). Pat O'Malley supplied Cyril's voice. Disney also made a few cartoon shorts that dealt with horses, such as *How to Ride a Horse* (1950) with Goofy and *A Cowboy Needs a Horse* (1956), but Disney usually reserved horses for live-action films.

Widowmaker starts Sluefoot Sue on her trip to the moon. (© Walt Disney Productions.)

119

Goofy teaches in *How to Ride a Horse* (1950). (© Walt Disney Productions.)

Pablito (Andres Valesquez) and his horse in *The Littlest Outlaw* (1955). (© Walt Disney Productions.)

The Disney movies or television films about horses often had several characteristics in common: the photography was excellent, the horses were beautiful and well trained, there was a strong bond between a youngster and a horse, kindness and love were all that was necessary to train horses, and discipline was never needed. Any youngster that tried to train horses using only the Disney approach would be in for a disappointment but the movies usually taught a lesson and were highly entertaining.

The first Disney horse feature film was *The Littlest Outlaw* (1955). A Mexican general hired a man to train his horse to jump for the big race. The trainer used cruel methods, and instead of improving, the horse became afraid of jumps. The general's daughter tried to force the horse to jump but he threw her, and the girl was seriously injured. The general ordered the horse to be killed. The trainer's young stepson, Pablito, knew that the horse had been abused, and he stole the horse and ran away. The horse escaped from the boy and was found by gypsies. The gypsies sold him for use in the bullfight arena as a lure for the bull. Pablito went to the bullfight, saw the horse in danger from the bull, ran into the arena, and rode the horse out by making a fantastic jump. Pablito and the horse returned to the general, who had realized his mistake, the horse had lost his fear of jumps,

Pablito (Andres Valasquez) is captured by bandits who threaten to steal his jumping horse in *The Littlest Outlaw* (1955). (© Walt Disney Productions.)

White Bull (Sal Mineo) and Tonka. (© Walt Disney Productions.)

and everybody was happy. Pedro Armendariz played the general, Rodolfa Acosta the trainer, Andres Velasquez was Pablito, and the horse was Conquistador, a member of the Mexican Equestrian Team. The film was also shown on the "Disneyland" television series as a two parter in 1958.

Tonka (1958) told the story of the U. S. Cavalry horse that survived Custer's massacre at Little Big Horn in 1876. According to Disney, a young Indian brave, White Bull (played by Sal Mineo), captured a magnificent wild horse that he named Tonka. An older brave, Yellow Bull, took the horse from White Bull. When White Bull saw the horse being mistreated, he set it free. Tonka was subsequently captured by wild horse wranglers and sold to the U. S. Cavalry. Captain Miles Keogh (Philip Carey) took the horse and named it Comanche.

White Bull snuck into the fort to see Tonka and was captured. However, he was released when Captain Keogh learned the reason that he entered the fort.

When Comanche was recovered after the massacre, a friend of the dead Keogh remembered that White Bull also loved the animal. Somehow White Bull, although he fought on the other side in the battle, was made an honorary trooper and put in charge of Comanche (Tonka). As mentioned earlier, one report claimed Tonka was played by television's Flicka.

But according to a Disney press release, Walt Disney selected a eight-year-old gelding named Canton to star as Tonka. Canton won the reining class at the San Francisco Cow Palace in 1956. He was trained by Charles Araujo. The press release also stated, "On completion of the filming of *Tonka*, the famous gelding was of-

121

Captain Miles Keogh (Philip Cary) and Tonka or Comanche in *Tonka* (1958). (© Walt Disney Productions.)

ficially retired to Disney's ranch near Palm Springs, California."

The real Comanche enjoyed a long life of leisure. General J. G. Wilson in 1897 wrote, "Comanche, a powerful horse nearly 16 hands, died at Fort Riley, Kansas on November 9, 1891. He was more than 30 years old. At Fort Riley, Comanche was daily saddled and bridled and led out for inspection but he never suffered the indignity of serving in the ranks. Captain Keogh was the last man to mount him." When Comanche died, he was mounted and exhibited at Chicago Colombia Exposition of 1893. Comanche was subsequently housed in a Fort Riley museum.

Miracle of the White Stallions (1963) was quite different from the other Disney horse movies. Leonard Maltin wrote, "*Miracle of the*

White Stallions is one of Disney's most unusual films, because it is so un-Disneyesque. The production, the story, the cast, the whole atmosphere of the production, give no clue that the Disney studio was behind it." The movie was based on the true story of the rescue of Austria's renowned Lippizan horses during World War II. Colonel Podhajsky, the head of the Spanish Riding School (played by Robert Taylor), managed to get some of the horses out of Vienna but the Stallions were taken to Czechoslovakia. The colonel convinced General Patton to rescue the stallions.

The film was also un-Disneylike in that it was not a success at the box office and the critics panned it. The *Time* critic wrote, "They [the horses] are more intelligent than most of the people connected with this picture."

The Horse in the Gray Flannel Suit (1968) was about a Madison Avenue advertising executive

122

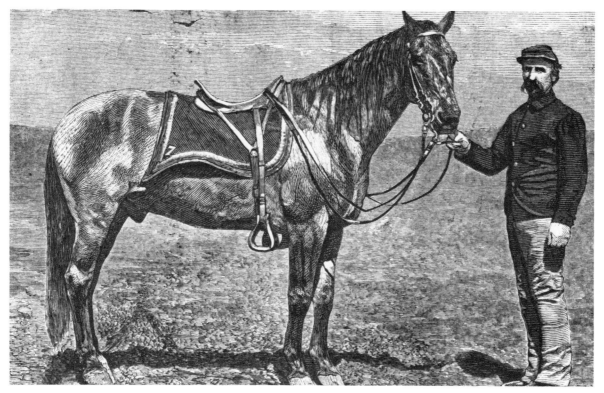

The real Comanche during his stay at Fort Riley.

Robert Taylor leads the prized stallions in *Flight of the White Stallions* (1963). (© Walt Disney Productions.)

Injun Joe came East and became Nautical, a member of the USET in *The Horse with the Flying Tail* (1968). (© Walt Disney Productions.)

who had two problems. The first problem was that he was having difficulty paying his bills, particularly at the riding stable where his horse-loving daughter (Helen) had managed to charge nine hundred dollars. His second problem was to find a way to promote a sour-stomach remedy. The executive, played by Dean Jones, talked his boss into buying a horse, naming it Aspercel after the patent medicine, and letting his daughter ride the horse. He convinced his boss that Helen and the horse would win a lot of shows and thus provide Aspercel with a great amount of publicity. As in many Disney movies, the father's plan didn't work out as expected. Helen couldn't stand the pressure of having to win in order for her father to keep his job. Suzie (Diane Baker), the owner of the riding stable, took over and won the big show with Aspercel. Jones kept his job, and payed off his bills. Diane Baker got Jones (who was a widower) and Helen got a horse.

The Horse with a Flying Tail (1961) was a featurette. A palomino colt named Injun Joe started life in a New Mexico village where he had to forage for food to survive. As a three-

year-old he was broken and trained as a cutting horse. An ex-cavalry officer bought him when he saw the horse's potential as a jumper. Injun Joe was then sold to a fox hunter in Virginia. During his East Coast adventures, he was selected for the United States Equestrian Team. Renamed Nautical, he proved to be an important member of the team and won a big match. The film was awarded an Oscar as the outstanding documentary feature.

The Tattooed Police Horse (1964) was foaled in Kentucky. Jolly Roger was a Standardbred of excellent breeding, and trainer Pam Churchill predicted that he would be a champion. He was entered in racing before being properly trained and broke stride in the home stretch. When it appeared that he couldn't be broken of this bad habit, he was ruled off the track. Jolly Roger was taken to Arizona but returned East when he was purchased for the Boston Police Force. Under Captain Hanley's training, Jolly Roger became an excellent police horse. One day Captain Hanley and Jolly Roger were called to a racetrack because of an accident. When Jolly

Jolly Roger, a trotter, became a member of the Boston Mounted Police Force in *The Tattooed Police Horse* (1964). (© Walt Disney Productions.)

124

The test of smoothness of gait is shown by Chago (Roberto Vigoreaux) when he balances a glass of wine on his head while riding his Paso Fino stallion in *Christobalito, The Calypso Colt.* (© Walt Disney Productions.)

dent and the owner's son, Silver (Jeff Tyler), tried to earn money by entering Chester in a pulling contest. Chester beat the other horses but lost to a tractor. On the way home from the contest, the boy and the horse found the lumber boss trapped in a burning truck. Silver attached a cable to Chester's harness and the big Belgian righted the cab so that Silver could get the boss out before the truck exploded. As a reward for their heroic effort, the boss asked Silver and Chester to report to work the next morning. Chester is owned by producer-director Larry Lansburgh. Lansburgh said, "Chester is really a large Belgian. He weights 2,200 pounds and stands over 18 hands tall. He is docile but strong. Chester has pulled over 3,500 pounds in dead weight in competitions at fairs and carnivals."

A television film starred a Paso Fino. Paso Fino means "fine walk," and the horses of that breed are noted for their unique walk. They

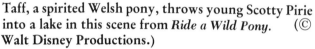

Taff, a spirited Welsh pony, throws young Scotty Pirie into a lake in this scene from *Ride a Wild Pony.*   (© Walt Disney Productions.)

Young Josie Ellison (Eva Griffith), although crippled, trains Bo to be her cart pony in *Ride a Wild Pony* (1976). (© Walt Disney Productions.)

have a lateral gait in which the hind hoof strikes the ground a fraction of a second before the front hoof on the same side. This gives the impression of the horse floating along. The gait is very comfortable for the rider and not tiring to the horse. In *Cristobalito, the Calypso Colt,* an orphan fruit peddler named Chago (Roberto Vigoreaux) accepted a job as stable boy for a wealthy Puerto Rican rancher. Chago became attached to a Paso Fino stallion named Cristobalito. Cristobalito was injured and the owner planned to have him put to sleep. Chago ran away with Cristobalito to his former village. The farmers cured and trained the stallion. In return for their help Chago and Cristobalito represented the villagers in the All Island Horse Championships.

A recent Disney equine feature film is *Ride a Wild Pony* (1976). Scotty Pirie (Robert Bettles) was the young son of a poor farmer living near a small Australian outback town. He loved ponies but he had none of his own, so he snuck into a rich neighbor's farm to ride one of his wild Welsh ponies. Scotty got into trouble with the foreman of the ranch and with the truant officer. The neighbor learned that Scotty needed transportation to get to school, and he offered to give him one of the ponies. Scotty's father, Angus (Alfred Bell), refused to accept charity but payed three pounds for the pony. Scotty rode the pony, which he named Taff, to school, but Taff got loose and stirred up the townspeople, upsetting carts and racing through the stores. One day Taff disappeared and Scotty made futile efforts to find him. In the meantime, the neighbor's young daugher, Josie (Eva Griffith), who was confined to a wheelchair, trained one of the ponies to pull her cart. She named the pony Bo, and he responded to her gentle treatment. Scotty saw Bo and claimed that he was Taff. He took the horse from the stable but the police caught him and it was decided that the court should determine the owner of the pony. It was found that the pony

Flash, the pit pony, and the three young co-stars of *The Littlest Horse Thieves* (1977), Chloe Franks, Benjie Bolgar, and Andrew Harrison. (© Walt Disney Productions.)

was the wild Taff when he was with Scotty but the gentle Bo when he was with Josie. Scotty took the pony home, but he and Josie became friends and he and the pony visited her.

The movie was filmed in the Horton Valley, four hundred miles northwest from Sydney. The ponies were supplied by Rupert Richardson, the president of the Welsh Pony Society in Australia. However, they were trained for the movie by Jim Prine, whom the Disney people brought in from California.

The Littlest Horse Thieves (1977) was set in a mining community in the north of England in the early 1900s. It told the story of the efforts of three children to save the lives of the "pit ponies." Pit ponies worked in the mines but they were no longer needed when machinery was brought into the mine. The ponies were to be slaughtered but the children steal the ponies from the mine. Eventually, the ponies are taken from the children and are about to be loaded on a van when an explosion traps ten men in the mine. The men are saved with the aid of Flash, the fourteen-year-old lead pony, but Flash loses his life.

The Disney Studios said, "Since pit ponies have a sturdy character particularly their own, several retired pit ponies were borrowed from a pony center in nearby Durham county. They had their own staff to look after their welfare and a Disney animal trainer to help them study for their film performances."

8
The Other Equines

The horse's relatives haven't received as much motion picture glory as the horse. Jeanette MacDonald sang "Donkey Serenade" in *The Firefly* (1937) and Claudette Colbert took a bath in asses' milk in *The Sign of the Cross* (1932), but mules and donkeys are usually regulated to being the mounts of sidekicks such as Festus of the "Gunsmoke," series or padres from the missions or to roaming the desert with crusty old prospectors. They were seldom the favorite of the cowboy hero in the Western movie. Of course, there were a few exceptions. Big Boy Williams rode a jackass, caught criminals, and saved the banker's daughter in *The Jack Rider* (1921). Tom Mix used a white mule to help catch narcotics smugglers and find a lost gold mine for the murdered owner's granddaughter in *The Drifter* (1929). In *The Rough Diamond* (1921) Mix lost his job as a ranch hand because he was caught singing during working hours. Therefore, he and his pet mule joined the circus.

Wallace Beery rode a mule in *Jackass Mail* (1942) and drove mules in *20 Mule Team* (1940). Douglas MacLean was locked in a safe by bank robbers in *Passing Thru* (1921). He was rescued when his pet mule kicked out the wall. Randolph Scott had a trick mule and pet lion cubs in *Man of the Forest* (1933). A donkey with a foal

saved John Wayne and his godson from death in the desert in *Three Godfathers* (1948). Burl Ives, as a wandering troubadour, rode a mule in *Sierra* (1950). *Two Mules for Sister Sara* (1970) starring Clint Eastwood really wasn't about two mules although Shirley MacLaine did ride one.

Clint Eastwood also rode a mule in *A Fistful of Dollars* (1966). When three men that

Mules and donkeys didn't get the representation in the Westerns that they deserved but they were frequently shown in the background, such as in the above scene from *The Cowboys* **(1972) with John Wayne and Slim Pickens.**

Eastwood wanted to kill laughed at the mule, Eastwood used the insult as an excuse to gun them down. Eastwood said, "My mule doesn't like people laughing. He gets the crazy idea your laughing at him. Apologize." Of course, they didn't and, of course, Eastwood shot all three of them before they could shoot him.

Bad Company (1972) had two mules named John Henry and Bonnie from the Myers and Well Stable. Roy Rogers had not only Trigger but also a burro in *Grand Canyon Trail* (1949).

Gene Autry starred in *Mule Train* (1950) and *Pack Train* (1955). Kirk Douglas and Dewey Martin rode mules from Kentucky to St. Louis in *The Big Sky* (1952). They sold the mules for twenty-eight dollars and joined a fur-trading expedition to the West.

But mules and donkeys (burros) did not get fair representation in the Western movies. They were more than novelties and were used by many people other than prospectors. Of course, it is true that a prospector was dependent on his "Rocky Mountain Canary." The burro carried tools, bedroll, food, water, and cooking utensils. Many stories have been told of how the burro helped the prospector find gold and of the love-hate relationship between them. The burro always managed to maintain a degree of independence.

For example, in a court case a defense lawyer called in a prospector as an expert witness. He asked the man how long he had been a prospector and the man replied, "For thirty years." In subsequent testimony, the prosecutor asked the man how much time he had been prospecting and the man replied, "Five years." The prosecutor thought he had trapped the witness in a lie and asked him why he had previously answered thirty years. The man replied that he had been a prospector for thirty years but had spent only five years prospecting and the other twenty-five years searching for his burro. The judge accepted his testimony as an expert witness.

Many people other than prospectors also used donkeys and mules. In 1869 Harvey Riley reported that he had seen Delaware, Potawatamies, Kickapoos, Pawnees, Cheyennes, Piutes, Sioux, and Arapahoes use pack mules. G. R. Vernam claimed that most Indians rated mules as particularly choice possessions

and went to great lengths to obtain them. Cheyennes, Kiowas, Arikaras, and Mandans were reported by French fur-trappers to have many mules. Many Indians, particularly those of the Southwest, used burros.

The mule was the favorite pack animal in the West. The mule trains could travel about twenty-five miles a day but were reported to go forty miles a day when the trail was good. Prior to 1850, California was the primary source of mules for the West. Historian E. F. Mack stated that many trading parties used the Santa Fe to Los Angeles trail to travel to California to purchase mules. Frequently, the traders would return to Santa Fe with as many as one thousand head. Mack claimed, "During the early history of the trail, mules were its raison d'etre in every sense of the word." In 1852 California had more than sixteen thousand mules valued at eight hundred thousand dollars. Most of them were used to pack goods to the miners. By 1855 the mule population of California was thirty-one thousand. Mules were also used to move freight to mine fields in other states. It was reported that in 1866 six thousand mules left Walla Walla, Washington, with freight for Montana. The army also had many mules. General George Custer had a large pack train of mules and so did General George Crook when he fought the

Mules were not only used in the winning of the West but also in later wars. Many were used in early World War II. The above photo shows some of the mules in Fourth Field Artillery in 1940.

Jim Garner convinces Lou Gossett that he should ride
the donkey in *Skin Game* (1971).

Apaches. Texas had 191,000 mules in 1880, but, of course, many of them were used in farming. Nevertheless, there was about one mule for every ten horses in the Western States in the post-Civil War period, and the movies didn't appear to show mules in that large of a ratio.

Some cowboys even preferred to ride mules to horses. The mule was not as fast as the horse but he usually had more endurance, could tolerate heat better, was more resistant to disease, and was widely thought to require less feed than the horse. The cowboys also had mule races. But although mules and donkeys perhaps did not get fair representation in the movies, they did have a few bright spots.

In *Brighty of the Grand Canyon* (1967) Old Timer (Dick Foran) made friends with one of the feral burros of the Grand Canyon and named him Brighty. Old Timer struck gold, but he was robbed and killed by Jake Irons (Pat Conway). Brighty went to the camp of the famous hunter Jim Owens (Joseph Cotton). Theodore Roosevelt (Karl Swenson) was visiting Owens. Brighty greatly impressed Roosevelt and Owens when he fought off a mountain lion. Brighty took Owens to Old Timer's gold mine, and Jake Irons was brought to justice. Brighty was played by Jiggs, a burro from Illinois. The movie was based on the book by Marguerite Henry, who also wrote *Misty of Chincoteague*.

There was a real Brighty of the Grand Canyon. He was probably born sometime in the 1880s and lived in the canyon for more than thirty years. He worked on projects such as the building of a suspension bridge across the Colorado River and became a favorite of the men of the National Park Service. He would spend the winters foraging for himself in the lower part of the canyon and return to the camps in the summer.

According to one report, Brighty was killed to provide meat by a fugitive from justice who was stranded in the Grand Canyon in a snowstorm.

A young boy's love for his pet burro was illustrated in *The Gallant One* (1964). A ten-year-old motherless Peruvian boy (Arturo) had to move in with his uncle when his father was unjustly jailed for robbery. The uncle sold the boy's pet burro to buy whiskey. Arturo searched for the donkey but the donkey was killed by a rabid mountain lion. Arturo's happiness was restored when his father was shown to be innocent, and released from prison, and the village priest gave Arturo another burro.

Bobby Breen had a mule for a friend in *Breaking the Ice* (1938). He sang, "Tellin' My Troubles to a Mule."

Jazbo, a donkey, was listed in the credits of *The Three Must Get Theres* (1922) a burlesque of *The Three Musketeers.*

Wild Burro of the West (1960) was a Disney television film about a burro roaming the deserts of southern California.

Bob Burns raised mules in *I'm From Missouri* (1939) and unsuccessfully tried to sell them to the British Army.

Young Ted Donaldson had a burro for a pet in *Personality Kid* (1946).

A seven-year-old Italian war orphan made his living by carrying small loads on his donkey Violetta in *Never Take No For An Answer* (1952). When the donkey became sick, the boy tried everything in his power to help the animal and finally went all the way to the Pope to get a cure.

Advertisement for *Brighty of the Grand Canyon* (1967).

The biggest long-eared star was Francis the Talking Mule, a star in seven Universal films from 1950 through 1956. The films never received great acclaim from the critics, but they were successful at the box office. Donald O'Connor was the bumbling friend whom Francis rescued in the first six films and Mickey Rooney was the bumbler in the seventh and last film. Chill Wills supplied the voice of Francis. Arthur Lubin was the director. He was also the director of the television series about a talking horse—"Mr. Ed." The Francis films were *Francis* (1950), *Francis Goes to the Races* (1951), *Francis Goes to West Point* (1952), *Francis Covers the Big Town* (1953), *Francis Joins the Wacs* (1954), *Francis in the Navy* (1955), and *Francis in the Haunted House* (1956).

Universal Studios generated a good deal of publicity looking for a mule to star in the Francis series. They staged a "beauty contest" in Columbia, Missouri, and took the winning mule to Hollywood. But the Missouri mule was demoted to being a stand-in when Jimmie Phillips of the Universal Animal Department found a California mule that was more photogenic and easier to handle. The mule was purchased for $350 and turned over to Les Hilton to be trained. Within two months Hilton had Francis ready for the movies. Threads were tied to the mule's lips or the jaws were moved by pressing a muscle on the side of the face to give the illusion of the mule talking. Francis performed the usual stunts such as climbing stairs and opening newspapers but he would not sit down. Stand-ins were used whenever sitting was necessary. Incidentally, Francis was really Frances. Her

Donald O'Connor, Martha Hyer, and Francis.

original name was Molly.

Scudda Hoo! Scudda Hay! (1948) starred Lon McCallister, June Haver, Walter Brennan, and two mules. The mules got good reviews but the movie didn't. The movie critic for *Time Magazine* wrote, "The leading roles in the movie are played by two of the most gorgeous henna hay-burners that ever plodded out of a studio make-up salon. The movie will probably make a big hit with mules and may also appeal to some children. Adult people and horses may resent the film's hee-hawed refrain: that mules are smarter than either of them." Bosley Crowther of the *New York Times* wrote, "They [the mules] are very pretty creatures—sleek and shiney and full of oats but the best they can do in way of action is pull a tractor out of the mud. And the most suspenseful element they can offer is a not too exciting uncertainty as to whether they will drive for Lon." Mr. Crowther probably never tried to drive mules or else he would have never called the uncertainty unexciting. What does "Scudda Hoo

Francis.

The mule that kicks 100 yard fieldgoals in *Gus* (1976).
(© Walt Disney Productions.)

Scudda Hay" mean? *Time* said it meant gee and haw in mulese. Crowther said it meant giddap.

The plot was that Snug (Lon McCallister) bought the mules Moonbeam and Crowder because Roarer McGill (Tom Tully) beat them when he couldn't get them to work for him. The mules eventually responded to Snug's care and Snug proved that the people who ridiculed him for buying the team were wrong. Incidentally, not all reviewers panned the movie. *Parent's Magazine* wrote, " . . . there's excitement aplenty and a climax that will have you holding your breath."

The most recent long-eared star is the field-goal kicker in the Walt Disney production *Gus* (1976).

The mule's co-stars were Edward Asner, Don Knotts, Gary Grimes, Tim Conway, Tom Bosley, and Dick Butkus. Johnny Unitas also ap-

Gus practices kicking soccer balls at his home in Yugoslavia in *Gus* (1976). (© Walt Disney Productions.)

peared. Hank Cooper (Edward Asner) owned the hapless California Atoms, a professional football team. Cooper's secretary, Debbie Kovac (Liberty Williams), read about a mule in Yugoslavia that could kick soccer balls the length of the field. Cooper imported the mule and his owner, Andy Petrovic (Gary Grimes), to perform at halftime. The mule was so impressive that in the next game Cooper put Gus in to kick a field goal. With Gus kicking one hundred-yard field goals, the team started to win. Despite being sabotaged by one of his own teammates (Dick Butkus) and attempted kidnappings by two inept con-men (Tom Bosley and Tim Conway), Gus managed to bring the team into contention for the Super Bowl. Gus was kidnapped on the day of Super Bowl game. Andy got Gus back in time for the last play of the game. Gus knew that Andy needed to prove himself, so he missed the ball completely and Andy picked it up and ran for a 106-yard winning touchdown. The movie was based on a story by Ted Key, the creator of "Hazel." The mule that played Gus was twelve years old, thirteen hands high, and weighed seven hundred pounds. He had appeared in many movies but never had had a starring role.

A Buena Vista publicity release said,

Despite the fact that mules and stars are supposed to be stubborn, temperamental creatures, Gus seldom complained during long hours of shooting.

"Mules are smart animals", says head trainer Bobby Davenport. "They're only stubborn when they're abused. When they've had enough, they just quit".

Gus never quit, but there was one time when he had had enough. During filming of a scene in a grocery store where Gus is being chased by would-be mulenappers Tim Conway and Tom Bosley, Gus was to step on several plastic mustard and ketchup containers and squirt Bosley in the face. Director Vincent McEveety, wanting everything to be perfect, kept having the scene done over. Gus co-operated through several retakes, but McEveety asked for yet another and immediately yelled "Cut!" Gus kept on trotting toward the camera.

Despite protestations from the production crew, the mule stomped the plastic bottles, spraying the directed and crew with the contents.

Then he turned to face them and gave a hearty "Hee-Haw!"

Bibliography

Amaral, A. *Movie Horses*. New York: Bobbs-Merrill Co., 1967.

Anon. "Animal Stars in the Movies." *Literary Digest* 85 (June 20, 1925): 54 60.

Anon. "Horse With a Message—Fury." *Time* 71 (March 10, 1958): 59, 60.

Austin, D. "Gunplay and Horses." *Films and Filming*. 10 (October 1968): 25.

Barbour, A. G. *The Thrill of it All*. New York: MacMillan Co., 1971.

Baxter, John. *Stunt—The Story of the Great Movie Stuntmen*. New York: Doubleday and Co., 1974.

Berton, P. *Hollywood's Canada*. Toronto: McClelland and Stewart., 1975

Brookshier, F. *The Burro*. Norma, Okla.: Univ. of Oklahoma Press, 1972.

Calder, J. *There Must be a Lone Ranger*. New York: Taplinger Publ. Co., 1975.

Cary, Dianna Serra. *The Hollywood Posse*. Boston: Houghton Mifflin Co., 1975.

Cawelti, J. *Six-Gun Mystique*. Bowling Green, Ohio: Bowling Green University Press, 1970.

Charles, Christopher. *"Those Marvelous Movie Horses."* *American Horseman*. Vol. 5 (April 1975):37

Christeson, Helen Mae, and Christeson, Frances Mary. *Tony and His Pals*. Chicago: Whitman, 1934.

Copper, Texas Jim. "Horses as Stars." *Films in Review* 22 (November 1971): 555.

Corneay, E. N. *Hall of Fame of Western Film Stars*. North Quincy, Mass.: Christopher Publ., 1969.

Dobie, J. Frank. *The Mustangs*. Boston: Little, Brown and Co., 1952.

Dudley, A. "Trigger." *Western Horseman* Vol. 14, no. 10 (1950), p. 60.

Elkin, Frederick. *The Child and Society*. New York: Random House, 1972.

Elliot, B. "Quarter Horses in the Movies." *Western Horseman* vol. 14, no. 7 (1950), p. 10.

Eyles, A. *The Western*. South Brunswick and New York: A. S. Barnes and Co., Inc., 1975.

Everson, W. K. *Pictorial History of the Western Film*. Secaucus, N. J.: Citadel Press, 1971.

Fenin, G. N., and Everson, W. K. *The Western*. New York: Grossman Publ., 1973.

Friar, R., and Friar, N. *The Only Good Indian*. New York: Drama Book Spec., 1972.

Griffith, R., and Mayer, A. *The Movies*. New York: Simon and Schuster, 1975.

Griswold, J. B. *"King of the Giddyaps"* (Buck Jones). "American Magazine" vol. 125, no. 1 (1938), p. 43.

Hart, William S. *My Life—East and West*. Boston: Houghton Mifflin, Co., 1929.

Hatley, G. B. "Run, Appaloosa, Run" *Appaloosa News* vol. 20, no. 7 (1966), p. 2.

Krafsur, R. P., ed. *The American Film Institute Catalog*. vol. F6 Feature Films in 1961-1970. New York: R. R. Bowker Co., 1976.

Lahue, K. C. *Winners of the West: The Sagebrush Heroes of the Silent Screen*. A. S. Barnes, N. Y. 1971.

Lahue, K. C. *Riders of the Range*. South Brunswick and New York: A. S. Barnes and Co., Inc., 1973.

Lee, Raymond. *Not So Dumb.* South Brunswick and New York: A. S. Barnes and Co., Inc. 1970.

Lewis, J. "Mustang—The Wonderful Horse World of Disney." *Horses and Horseman* 2(1974): 28 32.

Lewis, V. "Leo Carrillo, Rancher." *Western Horseman* vol. 15, no. 4 (1950), p. 18.

Lincoln, E. C. "Tony—The Horse With Fifty Million Friends." *Sunset Magazine* 57 (November 1926): 27.

Low, Rachael. *History of the British Film 1914-1918* Surrey, England, Univen Bros. 1948.

Mack, E. J. *Nevada,* Glendale Calif.: Clark Co., 1936.

Maltin, L. *The Disney Films.* New York: Crown Publ., 1972.

Manchel, F. *Cameras West.* Englewood Cliffs, N. J.: Prentice Hall Inc., 1971.

Martin, P. "I Call on Ben Hur." *Saturday Evening Post* 233 (August 20, 1960): 20.

Maynard, R. A. *The American West in Film: Myth and Reality.* Rochelle Park, N. J.: Hayden Book Co., 1974.

Munden, K. W., ed. *The American Film Institute Catalog.* Vol. F2. Feature Films 1921-1930. New York: R. R. Bowker Co., 1971.

McClure, A. F., and Jones, K. D. *Heroes, Heavies and Sagebrush.* South Brunswick and New York: A. S. Barnes Co., Inc. 1972.

McMurtry, L. "Cowboys, Movies, Myths and Cadillacs" *In Man and the Movies,* edited by W. R. Robinson. Baton Rouge: L. S. U. Press, 1967.

McNichols, C. L. "Picture Horse, The Styles in Movie Mounts." *Review of Reviews,* 95 (February 1937): 71.

McNichols, C. L. "Duke Goes to School" *The Horse* vol. 21, no. 6 (1940), p. 15.

Miller, Don. *Hollywood Corral.* New York: Popular Library, 1976.

Mix, Olive Stokes, and Heath, Eric. *The Fabulous Tom Mix.* Englewood Cliffs, N. J.: Prentice Hall, Inc., 1957.

Mix, Paul. *The Life and Legend of Tom Mix.* South Brunswick and New York: A. S. Barnes and Co., Inc.

Murphy, P. "Biography of a Champion." *Western Horseman* vol. 16, no. 10 (1951), p. 8.

Nachbar, J. *Western Films: An Annotated Critical Bibliography.* New York: Gardland Publ., 1975.

Parish, J. R. *Great Movie Series.* South Brunswick and New York: A. S. Barnes and Co., Inc. 1971.

Parkinson, M., and Jeavons, C. *Pictorial History of Westerns.* New York: Hamlyn, 1972.

Place, J. A. *The Western Films of John Ford.* Secaucus, N. J.: Citadel Press, 1973.

Pratt, G. C. Spell Bound in Darkness. Rochester, N. Y.: University of Rochester Press.

Reese, John. "Movie Horses are Real Hams." *Saturday Evening Post.* 228 (June 30, 1956): 42 43.

Riley, H. *The Mule.* Philadelphia: Claxton, Remsen and Haffelfinger, 1869.

Robertson, W. H. P. *The History of Thoroughbred Racing in America.* New York: Bonanza Books, 1964.

Rosa, J. G. "Buck Jones" *Western Film T. V.* Annual (1958), p. 43.

Self, Margaret. *The Complete Book of Horses and Ponies.*

Scott, Audrey. *I Was a Hollywood Stunt Girl.* Philadelphia: Dorrance & Co., 1969.

Smith, Ella. *Starring Miss Barbara Stanwyck,* New York: Crown Publ., 1974.

Smith, Helen. "Wm. S. Hart and Fritz." *Western Horseman* 38 (April 1973): 69.

Smith, Lewis. "Pinto Idols of Old. *Horse and Rider* vol. 14 (1975), p. 38.

Smith, Lewis. "The Horse the Stars Loved to Ride." *American Horseman* vol. 4, no. 7 (1974), p. 35.

Stimson, T. E. "Smart Actors." Popular Mechanics, 86 (September 1946): 97-104.

Tuska, Jon, "Retrospect: Ken Maynard" (in three parts). *Views and Reviews* vol. 1, no. 1 (1969), p. 6; vol. 1, no. 2 (1969), p. 23; vol. 1, no. 3 (1969), p. 22.

Tuska, Jon. *The Filming of the West.* Garden City, New York: Doubleday & Co.

Valentry, D. "Mister Ed." *Western Horseman* vol. 27, no. 6 (1962), p. 43.

Vernam, G. R. *Man On Horseback.* Lincoln, Nebraska: University of Nebraska Press, 1964.

Vernon, Arthur. *The History and Romance of the Horse.* New York: Dover Publ., 1939.

Wagner, R. "Beautiful and Dumb." *Colliers* 82 (December 22, 1928): 13-15.

Weiss, K., and Goodgold, E. *To Be Continued.* New York: Crown Publ., 1972.

Webb, Walter Prescott. *The Great Plains.* New York: Grosset and Dunlap, 1931.

Willet, R. "The American Western: Myth and Anti-Myth." *J. Popular Culture* 5 (1970): 455.

Zinser, A. *Seen Any Good Movies Lately.* Garden City, New York: Doubleday & Co., 1958.

Index